psychosocial
stress

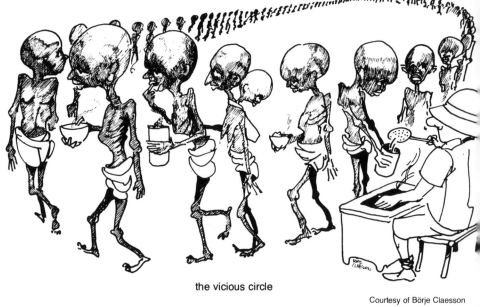

the vicious circle

Courtesy of Börje Claesson

psychosocial stress:

population, environment and quality of life

Lennart Levi and Lars Andersson

S P Books Division of
SPECTRUM PUBLICATIONS, INC.
New York

Distributed by Halsted Press
A Division of John Wiley & Sons

New York   Toronto   London   Sydney

Spectrum Publications, Inc.
86-19 Sancho Street, Holliswood, N.Y. 11423

Distributed solely by the Halsted Press Division of John Wiley & Sons, Inc.
New York.

Library of Congress Cataloging in Publication Data

Levi, Lennart.
  Psychosocial Stress
  "Originally published by Royal Swedish
Ministry for Foreign Affairs as a contribution to
the United Nations' World Population Conference"
held 1974.
  Bibliography: p. 108.
  Includes Index.
  1. Population—Congresses. 2. Human ecology
—Congresses. I. Andersson, Lars, Joint author.
II. Title.
HB85.L48   301.3   75-5808
ISBN 0-470-53105-3

Preface

Following the Economic and Social Council's Resolution 1672 (LII) the Swedish government in March 1972 appointed a National Preparatory Committee for the World Population Conference.

Within the frame of a small programme of scientific studies sponsored by the Committee, Lennart Levi, M.D., and Lars Andersson, B.A., were asked to give an overview of existing research on human response to environmental pressure.

One reason for this initiative was that the Committee felt that the medical aspects of the effects on human beings have not been sufficiently emphasized in earlier dicussion on the consequences of population growth.

The Swedish Preparatory Committee presents herewith the report to the United Nations World Population Conference.

Inga Thorsson

/Carl Wahren

Lars Jonsson

FOREWORD

I was very glad to learn that *Population, Environment and Quality of Life*, first published in a limited edition by the Swedish Government, will now be made available in a somewhat expanded, updated version to a world-wide readership by Spectrum Publications.

This study was originally sponsored by the Swedish National Preparatory Committee for the United Nations' World Population Conference in 1974 and, despite its limited printing, it became an immediate success, because the report was based on carefully documented data and dealt with both the theoretic and the practical aspects of some of the most pressing problems in contemporary society. Among these are: stress and disease due to deprivation or excess of sensory input, urbanization, ruralization, industrialization, economic and ecologic factors, the rapidity of social change, migration and uprooting, all of which have a decisive influence upon the quality of modern life.

There are few people, if any, who would be better qualified than Doctor Lennart Levi, Director of the Laboratory for Clinical Stress Research in Stockholm, and his collaborator, sociologist Lars Andersson to write a book of this kind. In fact, no one else has ever dared to attempt it.

I have known Doctor Levi for many years and because of our common interest in stress, I was able to convince him to lecture at our University on his important research. Furthermore, I recently had an opportunity to participate in several of his WHO sponsored symposia on 'Society, Stress and Disease' which took place in Stockholm. On these occasions I was deeply impressed by the fact that Lennart Levi is one of the rare contemporary scientists who has a good understanding of both the theoretic and the practical applications of the stress concept.

A thorough study of the present volume, and some of the many key references quoted in its carefully selected bibliography, will be of tremendous help to many. This book will render an invaluable service to humanity by enriching the Quality of Life through a better understanding of the problems of modern society and intimate interdependence of man and his total environment.

I was honored to be asked to write this brief foreword for a volume which certainly represents a great contribution to human welfare.

Université de Montréal   Hans Selye
Montréal, Canada

INTRODUCTION

The last few years have witnessed a rapidly increasing world-wide concern for current trends in the development of the total human environment and for their potential consequences, not only for the wellbeing, but even for the survival of the human race. Major areas of public concern comprise phenomena like the population explosion, environmental pollution, energy consumption and the resulting energy crisis, poverty, unemployment, famine, the prospect of nuclear, chemical, and bacteriological, and also "conventional" warfare, as well as more "every-day" phenomena, such as uprooting and rapid social change.

This book represents an attempt to compile what is known about some of these and other phenomena into an integrated picture as it relates to man's health, wellbeing and quality of life. A short synopsis of the various components of this ecosystem and some of their interrelationships might provide the reader with a bird's eye view of the entire pattern of problems and make it easier for him to consider each sub-problem and its potential solution in a holistic and ecological perspective.

"The Population Time Bomb"

The earth's population around the time of the birth of Christ was about 210 million. It took until 1825 to reach 1,000 million but the population then doubled after only another 105 years (by 1930). Since then the population has grown and covered the earth at an ever increasing rate—only 30 years later, by 1960, it had reached the 3 thousand million mark and 4 thousand million had been reached by the time the UN's World Population Conference finished, in other words in 1974, hardly 15 years later. By the year 2000 the world's population will be 6 to 7½ thousand million. A quarter of all the people who have *ever* lived since the dawn of history are alive today. If we do not alter the present trend, there will be approximately 50 thousand million people on the earth in 125 years' time.

Of the present population in the industrialized countries, 27 per cent is under 15 years of age. The corresponding figure for developing countries is 42 per cent. This situation is a population time bomb because these 1,000 million will shortly reach puberty. No matter what political measures one envisages regarding population, it is probable that the world's population will have reached 12 thousand million within our children's lifetime.

No Lack of Space

Despite these predictions there is still no real need to fear an actual lack of space on earth. The problems are of another sort; available food is not sufficient, sources of energy are limited, environmental pollution creates great problems, resources are unevenly distributed to an extreme extent, and at least 500 million people already live at or below starvation level. The situation already poses enormous medical, psychological and social problems and strains. Foreseen trends will aggravate these.

Forty-fold Increase in Urbanization

Population growth is only one cause (and one symptom) of these problems. Urbanization, migration to the big cities, is another important contributing phenomenon. Before 1800 there was not a single country in the world that was urbanized in the sense that half of the population lived in towns. Since then, however, the influx to the towns has increased at a colossal rate. Compared with a three-fold increase in total world population, urban population has increased forty-fold.

Present Day Migration

In the first half of this century alone, over 100 million people in the Northern Hemisphere have left or have been forced to leave their homes. Countless numbers have been deported or have fled from persecution.

Not all moves are permanent. Many countries import foreign labor on a more or less temporary basis. The number of so-called "guest workers" in West Europe is estimated at present to be 11 million. In addition to modern "migrations", there are innumerable moves within the borders of a particular country, *e.g.* about 20 per cent of the population of the USA moves house each year.

High Risk Groups:
The Very Young, the Old and the Handicapped

Some 42 per cent of the population in the developing countries is under 15 years of age. Millions of children live under extremely difficult conditions. During those years when sensitivity and vulnerability are greatest, hundreds of millions of children are subjected to poverty, undernourishment and neglect, often in extreme slum conditions. Moreover, the support, albeit imperfect, that the extended family provides is often lost by movement from rural areas to the cities' slum areas or by other population movements.

With a longer average life expectancy the number of elderly people in the population becomes ever greater, especially in industrialized countries (10 per cent over 60 years of age compared with 3 per cent in developing countries). This section of the community is also typified by a combination of increased vulnerability and increased exposure to the stresses in the environment. In developing countries social and medical care, for all practical purposes, is in the hands of the extended family. Countless numbers of old people are left without care and attention by the migration of the young and middle-aged to the cities.

A third high risk group comprises the physically, mentally and socially handicapped, *e.g.* the blind, the deaf, the crippled, the mentally disturbed, the sick, and those dependent on drugs or alcohol. We find yet again that the disastrous combination of increased vulnerability and increased exposure in industrialized countries as well as in developing countries, leads to various processes of exclusion from participation in everyday life.

These three main groups suffer most because of the environment and predicaments created by population increase and population movements. But wholly healthy individuals and groups can also suffer.

Environmental Problems that Aggravate this Process

Poverty

Statistics cannot bleed, and we have an unfortunate tendency to merely state without any real emotional involvement that a considerable proportion of humanity lives at or below the subsistence level. Large areas of the world, especially in Africa and Asia, have an annual gross national product (GNP) of only $200 (US), or less, per capita. The GNP is, of course, growing even in the developing countries, but at a much slower rate. than in the industrialized world. The gap between the rich and poor thus becomes ever wider.

Unemployment

Even today there are many hundreds of millions without work. The primary concern is capital-intensive rather than labor-intensive industrial and agricultural processes. The growth of population and the large proportion of children in today's population will cause the demand for new jobs—already huge in the present situation—to increase dramatically in the near future. The developing countries are going to need 1,000 million new jobs within the next three decades. These jobs will give a meaning to life, a human dignity and, last but not least, a chance to survive. But will they become available?

Famine

During the 1960's the world's production of foodstuffs has, on the average, increased by only 0.8 per cent per person per year. Furthermore, distribution is extremely uneven and the lack of foodstuffs in large areas of the world is glaring. Nearly 500 million people are undernourished. Hundreds of thousands of people have starved to death in Central and West Africa during the recent drought. We make half-hearted attempts at aid. An effective air lift of food supplies could have saved these lives, and a follow-up with comprehensive *help for self-help* would have offered them at least a modicum of quality of life in the long run. Our neglect to save these people will go down in history as one of mankind's *acts of passive genocide*.

Population, Environment and the Quality of Life

The authors argue for a view of the situation as a whole: medical, psychological, social and economic factors go together to produce interlocking pieces of a jig-saw puzzle, and an ecological and cybernetic view: the interplay between the complete individual and the complete environment is decisive for good health and well-being. The following is a brief resumé of the effect of the various relevant factors regarding population and environment, on the different aspects of the quality of life.

There is some—albeit inconclusive—evidence indicating that high population density, especially when it becomes still higher within a short time, produces discontent, aggressive behavior, alienation, and mental and psychosomatic illnesses. It is often stated that these apply especially to the slum areas of large cities, and when found in combination with unemployment, poverty and undernourishment. It is not clear whether it is high population density and/or life in the city itself which is of relevance as far as the effects leading to illness are concerned. Different investigations give contradicting results. The effects presumably depend to a great extent on the situation in which the high population density and/or urbanization process occurs. When it entails the uncontrolled movement of an uneducated, impoverished and undernourished rural population to the cities, together with a dramatic population increase and a breakdown of social welfare and the extended family's care of the sick and aged, there is no doubt that these processes lead to a decline in the quality of life and in health standards, often with a consequent threat to life itself.

What Can We Do?

Measures must be directed *simultaneously* towards acute situations (*e.g.* in Central and West Africa, Bengla Desh, etc.) and towards long-term development. It would be wrong to merely chip away at the rust while the boat sinks. It was at one time popular to smile condescendingly at the "Doomsday prophets" and their prophesies. The laughter is now stilled for the simple reason that doomsday, for millions of people, has already arrived or is imminent. In one African state alone, over 100,000 people have recently starved to death and countless more are still in the danger zone. With ever increasing population and extreme disparities in the distribution of resources, this is going to remain a reality and a challenge far into the future.

We have the necessary technology for saving the lives of these people. We also have the necessary resources. There are only two things lacking; wide-spread popular support and willingness on the part of the decision makers. We all have to realize that our relative passivity when it comes to throwing out the life-line, which we have within easy reach, will be considered by future generations as passive genocide. It must not be said of us in the wealthy countries of the world that we had the opportunity but that we left things as they were through our own egoism and smugness. However, long-term effort is equally important. This must be carried out simultaneously on many fronts. The present imbalance between population size and population growth in many parts of the world on the one hand, and resources and the increase of resources on the other, makes further effective family-planning an absolute necessity. This is of equal concern in industrial countries and in developing countries, the consumption of resources and pollution of the environment (per capita) being proportionally incomparably greater in industrial countries. A prerequisite is increased equality for women, improved education and a community alternative to the social welfare and care of the sick and old provided by the extended family.

The global production of foodstuffs (especially protein) must at the same time be increased and distributed to where it is most needed. The

UN's large-scale *Conference on the Human Environment* has shown as clearly as could be desired the extent of world-wide pollution of the environment and its dangers for the family of man. The explosive growth of urbanization, with its attendant flow of human masses into city slum areas, must be checked through development measures directed towards rural areas. Those who have already moved to the city must be helped if they are to attain a worthwhile human existence.

Worthwhile work is a fundamental human right. It is equally important to think about food for the soul as it is to think about food for the body. Although high mechanization or even automation of production in industry and agriculture is perhaps more profitable in short-term national economic planning, labor-intensive production is to be preferred in the light of the comprehensive view outlined here.

Each and every one of these and other relevant points contain an important *psychosocial* factor. This has been almost completely overlooked the world over in previous discussions. We find great pleasure in calling the reader's attention to an important document produced by the participants in the recent twenty-seventh World Health Assembly Technical Discussion (WHO, Geneva, May 1974; WHA 27/Technical Discussions/6), and its *three agreed bases* in considering the need and possibilities for international action in this field (*i.e.* psychosocial factors and health):

> (a) the importance of all aspects of the human environment, including the psychosocial and socioeconomic factors, for human health and man's well-being;
>
> (b) the increasing awareness that psychosocial factors can precipitate or counteract physical and mental ill health, profoundly modify the outcome of health action, and influence the quality of human life;
>
> (c) the resulting need for a holistic and ecological approach in social and health action and for the corresponding reorientation of medical and paramedical education and training.

Briefly, then, a plan of action is needed, an integrated plan for the world with regard to co-ordinated enterprises concerning large-scale family planning, action against pollution of the environment, planning with regard to the distribution of labor, social and medical planning, planning with regard to the production and distribution of foodstuffs, planning with regard to education and the teaching of work-skills, and planning for peace.

The Need for Evaluative Research

Many of these measures, no matter how well meant, can have undesirable effects. Those that may be desirable in economic planning may not necessarily be desirable in social and medical planning and vice versa. A continuous evaluation is necessary in order to safeguard humanity, as much in medical, psychological and social terms as in economic and technical ones. Only in this way can we discover where we are going and make the necessary corrections to the course we are taking. Only in this way can we maintain the preparedness necessary for taking constructive measures. Only in this way can we learn from our unavoidable mistakes.

The overriding consideration is not so much whether we can afford the above measures, but whether we can afford to leave things as they are.

This book was written at the request of the National Swedish Preparatory Committee for the UN World Population Conference and constituted part of the official Swedish input to this conference. This, however, does not imply any endorsement whatsoever by the sponsoring bodies. The material presented and the views expressed in this book are of course the sole responsibility of the authors.

The work was supported in part by the Swedish Medical Research Council (project No. B74-19P-4316-01).

Laboratory for Clinical Stress Research   Lennart Levi, M.D.
Stockholm, Sweden   Lars Andersson, M.A.

Table of contents

1 Delineation of the problem; definitions; scope of this document

1.1 The problem

The past few decades have seen a rapidly growing awareness of the exponential increase in the world population. There seems to be considerable agreement on the approximate *magnitude* of this increase within the next decades but very profound disagreement concerning its *effects* and the need for and design of possible *countermeasures*. Which are the present trends in population dynamics? Do they, indeed, alone or combined with present trends in environmental change, pose a threat to human survival? To wellbeing? To the quality of life? Many concepts, data and relationships in this area are ambiguous. Consequently, the primary objective of this document for the United Nations Population Conference 1974 is to define and clarify some of the key concepts, to describe present trends and projections, and to examine existing evidence of relevant relationships.

Some experts have regarded the entire problem as primarily a question of demography, focusing on numbers of births and deaths, disregarding the physical and psychosocial environmental setting. Others have allowed for present and future resources. Some have used human survival as their main criterion. Others have focused to various extent on aspects of levels of living and/or quality of life.

Depending upon their primary field of competence, authors tend to emphasize one or other of economic, medical, psychosocial, technological or ideological factors, paying some lip service to other factors but not taking them very much into consideration and not realizing that the outcome of population policies may differ considerably according to the set of criteria one chooses.

These brief introductory remarks are a reminder of the complexity of the problems under study. The present authors consider that whilst the analytical approach is an essential preliminary, the main view must be *holistic* and *ecological,* i.e. synthesizing as many aspects as possible of the man-environment system. The intention here is to bring together in one essay ideas from many disciplines concerned with the problem, so that decision makers, members of the public and scientists in various fields may have an idea of the roles of those aspects with which they are not familiar. No attempt has been made to be exhaustive in any one discipline, or to cover all aspects of this huge and complex field within the range of this document. The necessary demarcation with regard to the various components of the man-environment system can be summarized as follows.

In the present context we have regarded *levels* and *changes* in population density as a logical starting-point for our discussion. Accordingly we consider *high* and *low* population densities, as well as *increases* and *decreases* in population density. In the same context we also discuss *migration*, irrespective of whether or not it changes population density. Then we review some data on the world situation with respect to these variables and examine the assumption that they, indeed, do interfere with human wellbeing and quality of life.

It seems further reasonable to assume that man's reaction to such population dependant stimuli is conditioned to a very high degree by *individual and group characteristics.* Accordingly, the outcome in terms of quality of life may be very different for infants and old people as compared to young and middle-aged adults. Similarly, the outcome may vary considerably depending upon whether or not the target group is physically, mentally or socially handicapped. We therefore discuss the potential importance of such characteristics as age and handicap in considering various high risk groups.

Similarly, the resulting quality of life depends to a high degree on *characteristics of the environment* in which the process is taking place. These characteristics include urban and rural environmental settings. Environmental factors like climate, geographical conditions and technology may be of decisive importance.

Some additional *examples* of the importance of environmental factors may clarify this point. Crowding with close relatives as opposed to competitive strangers creates very different situations. *Economic* factors greatly modify individual and group reactions, inter alia because adequate economic resources make it possible to compensate for many potentially bad effects, e.g. by acquiring access to more and/or better space. *Cultural* factors strongly condition attitudes towards strangers, family planning and social responsibility as well as social interaction in the nuclear and extended family and in other groups. They also influence female and male roles and relationships, age of sexual début, attitudes towards legal and illegal abortion, social and health services, etc.

Our *end-point* comprises various aspects of the *"quality of life".* This concept has many components. Attempts can be made to find primarily "objective" criteria like those usually included in the "level of living" concept (education, employment, economy,' housing conditions, nutrition, etc). Important as these may be, we consider that equal emphasis should be put on more "subjective" criteria of physical, mental and social wellbeing, i.e. on *health as defined by the World Health Organization* ("not only the absence of infirmity or disease but also a state of physical and mental and social wellbeing"), cf. also page 16. This should comprise various aspects of the *man-environment fit,* i.e. satisfaction of needs, and congruency between expectations and perception of reality.

In considering these and other criteria, we fully recognize that they can and often do conflict. When considering good or bad effects, one must always be prepared to answer questions like: Good (or bad) for whom? In which context? In what respects? When? Failure to consider this and the entire pattern of complex interactions is probably one explanation for much of the confusion and controversy in this field.

Eventually we intend to focus on the need for *monitoring,* the prospects and need for *social action now,* and the need for combining such action with *evaluative research.*

The views expressed in this document are the sole responsibility of the authors and do not necessarily represent the opinions of the Swedish National Committee or the Swedish Government.

The authors wish to express their gratitude to Drs. *Gösta Carlestam* (physical planning) and *Aubrey R. Kagan* (epidemiology) for constructive criticism and much valuable information. Moreover, this review draws heavily on two recent documents, of which they are co-authors.[1, 2] The authors have contributed to this book in their capacities as scientists in psychosocial environmental medicine and sociology, respectively. They clearly recognize the contributions made by many other disciplines, and have tried to include them in this review, without, however, having been able to give the proper references on each specific point. For a complete list of all references used in one way or another, the reader is referred to pp. 108–130.

Briefly, then, we have attempted to cover a huge, complex field, using as our end-point a concept (quality of life) which may seem vague and ill-defined. We are very much aware of the difficulties but see this as a beginning, as an early step in an important direction. We therefore welcome criticism, suggestions and other feedback from our readers.

[1] Carlestam, G. and Levi, L.: Urban Conglomerates as Psychosocial Human Stressors – General Aspects, Swedish Trends, and Psychological and Medical Implications. A Contribution to the United Nations' Conference on the Human Environment. Royal Ministry for Foreign Affairs and Royal Ministry of Agriculture, Stockholm, Sweden, 1971.

[2] Kagan, A.R. and Levi, L.: Health and environment – psychosocial stimuli. Social Science and Medicine, 1974 (in press). Also published as Report No. 27 from the Laboratory for Clinical Stress Research, Stockholm, 1971.

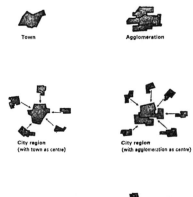

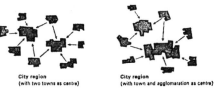

Figure 1. Diagrammatic explanation of the concepts town, agglomeration, city region and urban zone. (Source: Regional Planning: A European Problem. Council of Europe, 1968.)

1.2 Some definitions.

First we define some of our terms.

Urbanization: By urbanization we mean the process leading to a societal change characterized by the movement of people from rural to urban areas. As a consequence of this process, rural areas are depopulated while urban areas become increasingly densely populated, constituting towns, agglomerations, city regions, and urban zones (figure 1, cf. also Carlestam and Levi, 1971).

Density, areal and dwelling: A distinction is drawn between areal density and dwelling density. By areal density we mean unit per area indicators (such as people per sq.km.) and by dwelling density we refer to the number of individuals per living space within dwellings.

Crowding: A further distinction is drawn between the physical condition, density, defined purely in terms of spatial parameters, and the experience of crowding, a motivational state aroused through the interaction of spatial, social and personal factors, and directed toward the alleviation of perceived spatial restriction (Stokols, 1972 a). According to the proposed distinction, density is viewed as a necessary antecedent, rather than a sufficient condition, for the experience of crowding.

Migration: By migration is meant here movement from one country or region, and settlement in another, i.e. intercommunity residential change (and not just local moving).

Psychosocial stressors: These are stimuli suspected of causing disease which originate in social situations (i.e. in the environment) and affect the organism through the medium of higher nervous processes (Kagan and Levi, 1974).

Mechanisms: These are reactions in the organism conditioned by man's psychobiological "program" and induced by psychosocial and other stimuli which, under some conditions of intensity, frequency or duration, and in the presence or absence of certain interacting variables, will lead to disease (Kagan and Levi, 1974).

Stress: This is the non-specific response of the body to any demand made upon it, a stereotyped, phylogenetically old adaptation pattern, primarily preparing the organism for physical activity, e.g. fight or flight (Selye, 1971; Levi 1972 a). These "stone age" stress reactions, which may be provoked by a variety of psychosocial and other conditions of modern life, where no physical action is possible or socially acceptable, have been suspected of eliciting physical and mental distress or malfunction, and eventually even structural damage. Briefly, then, stress is one of the mechanisms suspected of leading to disease. This *biological* stress concept differs from the concept used in *physics* (where stress is referred to as an applied force or system of forces that tends to strain or deform a body), and from various analogies used in psychology and sociology (cf. Levi, 1971).

Precursors of disease: These are malfunctions in mental or physical systems which have not resulted in disability but which, if they persist, will do so (Kagan and Levi, 1974).

Disease: Disease is disability caused by mental or somatic malfunction. Disability is failure in performance of a task. This must always include tasks considered essential, might include tasks considered normal, and, when more is known, will include tasks that are considered optimal. In applying this definition it is necessary to know from whose point of view it is to be applied and to state the level of the biological hierarchy to which it refers. Disease as defined is different at the cell, organ, and organism level (Kagan and Levi, 1974).

Quality of life: By this we mean a composite measure of physical, mental and social wellbeing as perceived by each individual and by each group, and of happiness, satisfaction and gratification (cf. Campbell and Converse, 1970). Measures can concern overall as well as component life satisfaction, involving areas like health, marriage, family, job, housing, financial situation, educational opportunities, self-esteem, creativity, competence, belongingness and trust in others.

Interacting variables: These are intrinsic or extrinsic factors, mental or physical, which alter the action of "causative" factors at the mechanism, precursor, or disease state. By "alter" we mean they promote or prevent the process that might lead to disease (Kagan and Levi, 1974).

1.3 A theoretical model for the study of population, environment and quality of life

A systematic study and discussion of the interrelationships, if any, between high, low, increasing and decreasing population density and migration, and individual and group characteristics on the one hand, and quality of life on the other, as conditioned by interacting environmental influences, is facilitated by the use of a simple ecological model (figure 2).

To the left in the model (box 1) we find *population structures* and *processes* like density and change, and migration.

These give rise to a number of physical and psychosocial *stimuli* (box 2) acting on individuals and groups.

The human organisms exposed to these stimuli have a number of characteristics, e.g. age, sex, physical and mental status etc., determined by genetic factors and earlier environmental influences. The resulting *"psychobiological program"* (box 3) determines the organism's propensity to react in response to various stimuli.

The interaction of the stimuli, the psychobiological program and the interacting variables (see below) determines the *reactions* displayed by the individual or the group. Some of these reactions may be nonspecific in the sense that they are provoked by almost any stimulus and/or in almost any individual, i.e. stress as defined above (cf. Selye, 1971; Levi, 1972 a). Others are more specific. Some of the reactions, interesting as they might be from the viewpoints of basic sciences, do not relate to various aspects of quality of life, directly or indirectly, whereas others

A Theoretical Model for the Study of Population, Environment and Quality of Life

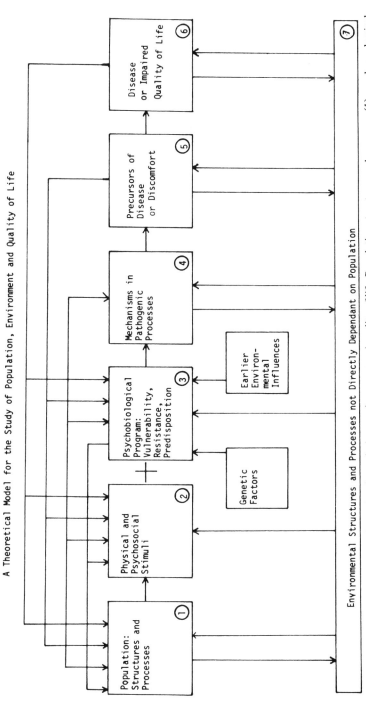

Figure 2. A theoretical model for the study of population, environment and quality of life. Population structures and processes (1), produce physical and psychosocial stimuli (2). Their interaction with man's psychobiological "program" (3) and with environmental structures and processes not directly dependant on population (7) determines the psychological and physiological reactions [mechanisms (4), e.g. stress] of each individual. These may, under certain circumstances, lead to precursors of disease or discomfort (5) or to disease or impaired quality of life (6). The sequence is not a one-way process but constitutes part of a cybernetic system with continuous feed-back.

17

do. The latter comprise physiological *mechanisms* (box 4) such as neuroendocrine hyper-, hypo-, and dysfunction, anxiety, depression and distress. (Using a sociological instead of a medical frame of reference, these might be replaced by phenomena like aggression, alienation, and social apathy and disintegration.)

The mechanisms are known or suspected to cause *precursors* of disease or discomfort (box 5), or *disease* or impaired quality of life (box 6).

Predisposing *interacting variables* (box 7) may promote this sequence of events, and protective interacting variables may counteract it (e.g. economy, physical environment, nutrition).

As already emphasized, the model is ecological. This implies that the process just described is not a one-way flow but constitutes a cybernetic process with continuous feedback. Accordingly, if disease (or social disintegration) has occurred in an individual (or a group), this has repercussions back on population density and change variables (box 1), individual and group characteristics (box 3) and on interacting variables (box 7).

Our task now is to describe as far as possible the contents of each "box" and the relationships, if any, between the various boxes, using *population density* and *change* and *migration* as a starting point and *quality of life* as a logical endpoint.

1.4 Some general comments on potentially pathogenic environmental stimuli and their relation to human wellbeing

1.4.1 Deprivation and excess

The evidence that environmental *physical* stimuli can cause disease – in the sense that exposure, avoidance or manipulation of them increases, decreases, or removes the chance of becoming ill or reverses ill health when it occurs – is established for a large number of factors and diseases.

The role of extrinsic, *psychosocial* stimuli is not so clear. In an attempt to review present knowledge, we shall consider what is known of the relationships between psychosocial stimuli and quality of life in terms of

☐ mechanisms;
☐ precursors of disease;
☐ disease itself.

Examples to clarify the use of these terms will be given below but it should be said now that although factors can often be categorized according to the above definitions, there are many occasions when the

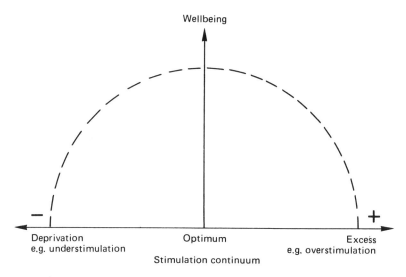

Figure 3. Theoretical model of the relationship between wellbeing and various levels of stimulation. Deprivation of stimuli as well as excess is accompanied by a decrease in wellbeing.

category is not clear or when categories are interchangeable. Nevertheless, we think this will facilitate discussion and probably lead to a better understanding of the problems. Where possible, we will indicate whether this relationship is certain, probable, or speculative.

The variety of situations through which man is exposed to psychosocial stimuli is almost infinite. In the present context we attempt to delineate certain classes of situations and stimuli that are suspected of exerting a negative influence on various indices of the quality of life.

Such stimuli arise from *excess* as well as *deprivation* of most environmental factors (e.g. parental care, communication, ambiguity, freedom of action, security, population density, sensory stimulation and environmental change). The assumption is that these and other environmental factors are likely to have an inverted u-shaped relation to wellbeing (figure 3). Thus, a certain amount of social change, parental care and sensory stimulation is advantageous, whilst lesser or greater amounts may be harmful. The optimal amount obviously varies between individuals, the environmental potential for decreasing the quality of life being a function of the degree of *incongruence* between individual and group *abilities* and *needs* and the environmental *demands* and *opportunities*. Equally important is the magnitude of incongruence between individual and group *expectations* and *perceived reality*.

1.4.2 Physiological mechanisms, and precursors of disease

There is much animal and human experimental evidence on the effect of psychosocial stimuli on physiological *mechanisms*. Most of this evidence with respect to neuroendocrine mechanisms relates to the (1) hypothalamo-adrenomedullary and (2) hypophyseal-adrenocortical axes, with increased secretion of (a) adrenaline, (b) noradrenaline, (c) corticosteroids and (d) thyroxine (for explanations of these and other medical terms, see Glossary, p. 131). Although there are probably many other mechanisms, these have been considered particularly relevant and studied most. Recent reviews of present knowledge in this field are to be found in Levi (1971 a and 1972 a) and in Kagan and Levi (1974).

Some of the physiological changes evoked psychosocially elicit signals in turn to the cerebral cortex. Under certain circumstances, even "normal" signals of this type may be *interpreted* by some individuals as symptoms of disease (as in the case of hypochondriasis, e.g. the normal beating of the heart is experienced as "palpitations" and interpreted as a symptom of heart disease). If the psychosocial stimulation exemplified above is pronounced, prolonged, or often repeated, and/or if the organism is predisposed to react because of its psychobiological "program" or because of the presence or absence of certain interacting variables, the result may be a *hyper-, hypo- or dysfunction* in one or more organs and organ systems. Examples of such reactions are tachycardia and palpitations, vasovagal syncope, pain of vasomotor or muscular origin, hyperventilation, increased or decreased gastrointestinal peristalsis, etc. These reactions may or may not be accompanied by unpleasant emotional reactions like anxiety, depression, apprehension, etc. Depending on the type of reaction which dominates the clinical picture, one may speak of "psychoneurotic" or "organ neurotic" reactions, respectively. There is no sharp borderline between "normal" reactions on the one hand and hypochondriac, psychoneurotic and organ neurotic reactions on the other. The distinction probably has more to do with the quantity than the quality of the reaction. Besides, the accepted level where normality ends and disease begins is heavily influenced by cultural factors. For reviews of evidence concerning the reactions described above, the reader is referred to e.g. Dunbar (1954), Tanner (1960), Roessler and Greenfield (1962), Wolf and Goodell (1968), Lader (1969), Levi (1971 a and 1972 a), and Kagan and Levi (1974).

Further, psychosocial stimuli probably also influence health by impeding recovery and aggravating disability, whatever the etiology of the primary disease. Such a psychosocially induced *emotional overlay* may be rooted in, for instance, an intense anxiety about the disease, or in a utilization of the disease as a means of avoiding responsibility, justifying one's incapacity and providing a release from social pressure.

It is often postulated that the development of psychosocially induced disease is preceded by a "precursor" state characterized by malfunction of mental and physiological systems without apparent disability. This probably applies to mental processes, as in the case of relatively mild anxiety or depressive reactions, as well as to somatic processes, e.g. mild hypertension, glucose intolerance.

Sometimes the symptoms may be manifested in a mild to moderate disintegration of group behaviour.

As mentioned in connection with the definitions, it is sometimes impossible to demarcate the mechanisms from the precursors of disease or from disease itself. This is particularly so when, in clinical practice, the mechanism and, more often, the precursor, is given the disease label, e.g. "gastro-intestinal distress". Therefore, most of what has been said above concerning the relation between psychosocial stimuli and mechanisms, also applies to precursors and sometimes to disease itself.

In summary, associations between psychosocial factors and changes that are likely to be precursors of disease are established or suspected under certain conditions. It is probable that these precursors arise in real life situations as a result of psychosocial factors and that they can proceed to disease.

1.4.3 Stress and disease

According to these speculations, the human organism's pattern of response to a wide variety of environmental situations constitutes a phylogenetically old adaptational process ("stress" in Selye's sense), preparing the organism for physical activity, usually for fight or flight. However purposeful these activities may have been in the dawn of history, they seem to be inappropriate for the adaptation of modern man to the endless number of socioeconomic changes, social and psychological conflicts, and threats involved in living in developing and developed countries alike. Furthermore, for social reasons, man has to repress many of his emotional outlets and motor activities. This creates a situation which may very well involve disharmony between the expression of emotion, the neuroendocrine concomitants of emotion and the psychomotor activities likely to accompany such emotion. For example, modern man may feel anxiety or aggression in a marital or occupational setting without this showing in his facial expression or verbal or gross motor behavior. Situations do occur where man is compelled to exhibit emotional expressions and to perform physically or verbally in a way that is grossly incongruous with his actual neuroendocrine and emotional state. It is suspected that if this "stress" pattern of response to psychosocial stimuli and/or this psychophysiological discrepancy lasts long enough, it may be pathogenic. Indeed, processes of this kind have been claimed as a major factor in the etiology of several diseases in the field of internal medicine (for a review, see Levi, 1971 a).

1.4.4 Life change and health change

It has further been assumed that *life changes* — including those more or less related to population density and change — confront the human organism with the necessity to adapt, and that the organism reacts to this with the same old preparation for increased physical activity that has been described to occur when facing conditions requiring fight or flight. Holmes, Rahe and others (cf. Rahe, 1972 and 1974; Cleary, 1974) have demonstrated that the greater the number and intensity of changes in a subject's life over a certain period, the higher is his risk of undergoing a subsequent decrease in health status. The life changes mentioned by these authors also include a number of events clearly related to the main theme of this document, like engagement, marriage, pregnancy, gain of a new family member, marital separation, death of close family member, change in living or working conditions, revision of personal habits, etc.

A considerable number of recent studies support this relationship between amount of life changes and subsequent health changes, e.g. Theorell (1970), Theorell and Rahe (1971), Rahe and Paasikivi (1971), and Rahe and Lind (1971). Levi (1972 a) proposed "stress (Selye)" as the non-specific mechanism explaining this relationship — life changes act as stressors provoking "stress (Selye)", thereby increasing the rate of wear and tear in the organism and eventually leading to a rise in morbidity and mortality. — In a longitudinal study lasting 2–4 months on 21 male patients who had recovered from myocardial infarction, Theorell et al. (1972) demonstrated a positive, significant correlation between the individual weekly mean "scores" of life change and an index of "stress (Selye)" — the 24 hour level of catecholamine excretion — on the penultimate day of the same week. It may be hypothesized that this increase in catecholamine excretion reflects an increased sympathotonia, which in turn might lead — or otherwise be related — to several other potentially pathogenic mechanisms. In Theorell's (1970) cases, those exposed to most life changes were most likely to die.

The causal relationship between exposure to psychosocial stressors and subsequent disease is supported by numerous studies. Recent reviews will be found in Levi (1971 a) and Kagan and Levi (1974).

Briefly, then, a general concept of *psychosocially mediated ill health* is that a wide range of environmental situations (such as those related to population density and change) may engage a relatively small number of pathogenic physiological mechanisms, which may lead to precursors of a large variety of diseases and eventually to the diseases themselves.

Social situations are particularly likely to elicit pathogenic mechanisms when they are newly experienced and when natural or cultural protection is not available to the recipients. That is why present *rapid changes* in the environment relevant to fundamental activities such as

☐ child bearing and rearing;
☐ male-female roles and relations, and family life;
☐ work conditions;
☐ individual-leader communication;
☐ other man-environment interaction (industrialization, urbanization, housing, etc),

beneficial as they may be in some respects, are likely to be a potent hazard to health in developed and developing countries alike. All of these social changes are inherent in various population densities and changes.

2 Stimuli generated by population structures and processes

2.1 World population: past and present situations; future trends

Before discussing the possible *impact* of population density and change in urban and rural settings, the present *situation* and *trends* ought to be considered.

According to estimations published in connection with the second UN World Population Conference (United Nations, 1967, volume II), the world population around zero A.D. was 210 millions. The 500 million level was reached round 1625 and the one billion level came about 200 years later (1825). Thus, it took more than 1,800 years for the world population to increase from 210 millions to one billion. The second billion came much more rapidly, about 105 years later (1930), and the third billion was reached after only another 30 years (about 1960). It is estimated that we are now approaching the fourth billion which will be reached during the World Population Year, i.e. after some 15 years. The projections for the year 2000 predict a world population of somewhere between 6 and 7.5 billions, and around the year 2100, the population would reach the 50 billion level with the *present* rate of population increase.

The estimates for all periods are of course very rough and 20-year demographic forecasts in the past have seldom been validated by events. But even an error of, say, 100 million does not alter the picture to any considerable degree.

But the world picture is in no way uniform. In no less than 56 of 66 nations from which we have relatively reliable statistics (admittedly a biased sample), fertility is decreasing (Nature, 1972); in general, however, it is still very high. At the same time, mortality is declining almost universally due to improved nutrition and health services. The net result is an increase in world population, referred to by some authors as the *population explosion* (figure 4).

Population development has passed through the three stages of (1) high fertility/high mortality, (2) high fertility/low mortality, and (3) low fertility/low mortality. The entire sequence, which has reached different stages in different parts of the world (cf. figure 5), is usually referred to as the *demographic transition*. The first and last stages are characterized by low population growth, whereas the second stage is one of rapid

24

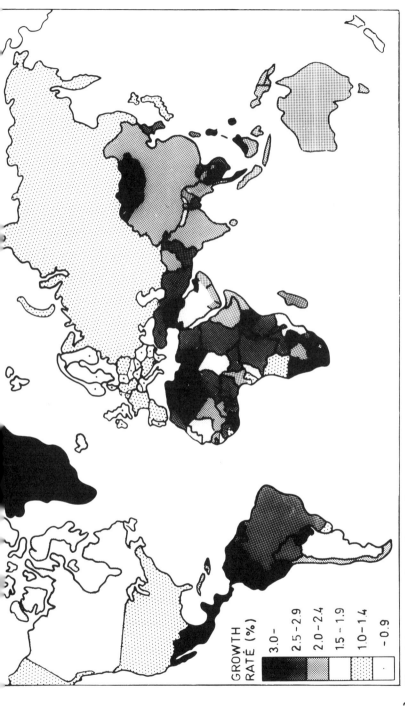

Figure 4. Average annual growth rates of population, by country 1960–1970. (Sources: World Bank 1973; United Nations 1971 a.)

GROWTH
RATE (%)

3.0 –

2.5 – 2.9

2.0 – 2.4

1.5 – 1.9

1.0 – 1.4

– 0.9

growth. This second stage now prevails in many of the developing countries and is, accordingly, influencing the entire world.

The second stage is said to be generated by a combination of *"revolutions"*, including 'the *agricultural* revolution, the *commercial, industrial, scientific* and *technological* revolutions, all resulting in the *"vital revolution"*, i.e. a pace of growth without precedent in longsettled areas. Briefly, then, the vital revolution is a relatively recent phenomenon and its general recognition as a global threat is even more recent.

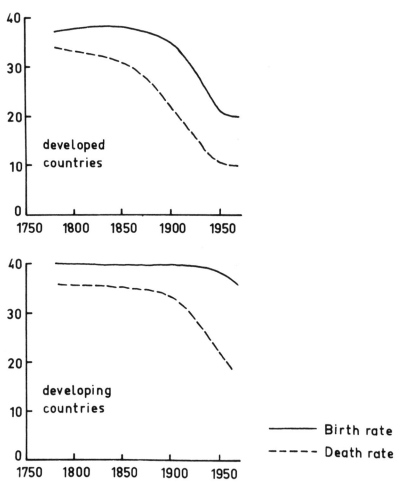

Figure 5. The mechanism of the demographic transition; smoothed curves. (Source: United Nations 1971 c.)

Clearly, population growth could be affected not only by various family planning measures but also by e.g. education, a higher age of marriage, greater equality for women and better economic living standards. As environmental factors influence population growth and the latter in turn influences environmental factors with a continuous positive or negative feedback, predictions are exceedingly hazardous. On the one hand, there is a considerable risk of vicious circles; on the other, social action or spontaneous development may intervene and change the trend.

Whatever these interventions may be, all demographic experts agree that there is a considerable lag before countermeasures take effect, because a high proportion of the total population is at present under 15 years of age. Consequently the number of couples in fertile ages will increase dramatically within a few decades whatever the outcome of present attempts at more efficient population planning and even with an increase in the present abortion rate. Already, the total number of illegal abortions in the world is said to exceed 30 million a year, to which may be added almost 10 million legal abortions. If this is true, it means that nearly 8 per cent of all "fertile" women in the world undergo abortion each year (Djerassi, 1972).

In view of the above, *predictions for the future* are naturally very approximate. As already emphasized, they cannot be based on purely mathematical calculations.

It is also well known that the manner in which data are presented can be used to arouse or subdue emotions in the lay reader, as illustrated in the two — identical — diagrams in figure 6.

No one seriously believes that these or other mathematical games actually predict the future. But with almost any prediction, it seems clear that the world — saving an unforeseen disaster — will face a rather dramatic rise in population density during the next 50 years.

As far as *space* is concerned, today's population increase does not create immediate problems — there is plenty of room on earth. Even in the foreseeable future, there will be large areas that are populated sparsely or not at all. Urban areas occupy only a few per cent of the total surface of the earth, although the surrounding area influenced by cities and the utilization of natural resources is considerably larger. However, population density problems are not confined to the question of space. The immediate *physical* limitations comprise availability of food (especially protein) and energy, and problems posed by pollution. The immediate *psychosocial* limitations are the absence of rules of conduct in the new social situations imposed by population changes.

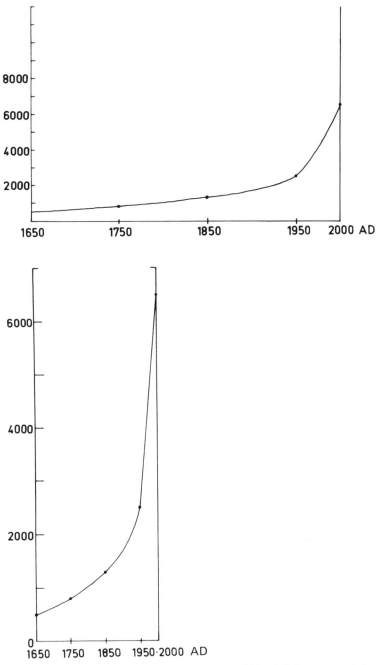

Figure 6. World population in millions. Presentation of identical data on population growth to subdue (top) or arouse (bottom) emotions in the lay reader.

28

2.2 Levels of population density

Some of the impressive rates of population *growth* given in the previous paragraph must be seen in the light of the present *density*. Although population *growth* is very considerable in many developing countries, population *density* is often relatively low. This applies to many countries in Africa and in South America (see figure 7), where huge areas are relatively sparsely inhabited. The population density per unit of total land area in many Asian countries is less than in western Europe, while in the large countries of Africa and Latin America it is about the same as in such "empty" countries as Sweden, the United States and the Soviet Union.

Relatively few areas in the developing countries are as densely populated as e.g. Belgium, The Netherlands, Southern England and the Atlantic coast of the United States. But such areas do exist, e.g. the Nile Valley with a population density of 800 inhabitants per sq.km. For comparison, the population density in Sweden varies from 3 inhabitants per sq.km. in the north to 138 in the south (1965). Briefly, then, population growth must be related to the area of the country, the present number of inhabitants and the environmental characteristics.

As emphasized in the paragraph on definitions, a high population density does not necessarily result in *crowding*. An example of conditions which probably but not necessarily lead to crowding is given by Dohrenwend and Dohrenwend (1974) in their discussion of living conditions in Hong Kong, the city which no doubt has the highest residential densities ever known in the world, se page 85.

Similarly, a United Nations Mission on Housing reported in 1965 that at the very high occupancy ratio of three or more persons per room, 49 per cent of all urban African households were overcrowded (cf. also United Nations, 1973b). Approximately half of Nairobi's population in Eastlands (excluding Uhuru, Harambee, and Outer Ring Road Estate), Kibera, Mathare Valley and Eastleigh were living at average occupancy rates of 3.3 to 6.3 persons per room. In contrast, it can be mentioned that there is no region in Sweden where more than 3 per cent of the households have an occupancy rate of more than 2 persons per room (SOU 1974:1). The above are examples of high and low dwelling density. To our knowledge, no worldwide data of this kind are available.

International discussion of population has focused to such an extent on "high" density that the disadvantages of "low" extremes tend to be forgotten. However, huge areas of the world are extremely sparsely populated, with people living in very small groups, often not more than one family. As pointed out by Querido (1964), such a situation

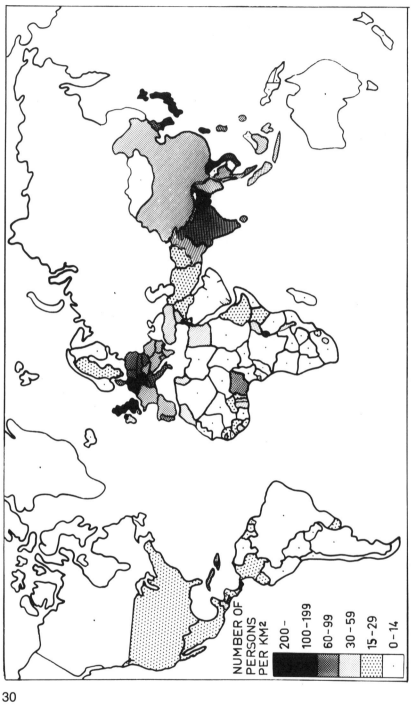

NUMBER OF
PERSONS
PER KM²

■	200 –
▨	100 – 199
▦	60 – 99
▨	30 – 59
░	15 – 29
□	0 – 14

30

constitutes an instance in which the individual members of a society can be dispersed to such a degree that the population density has fallen below a critical point. Mutual support has become impossible; communication between society members breaks down, and the transfer of knowledge and traditional and cultural lore is impeded.

2.3 Changes in population density

2.3.1 Some general considerations.

Changes in population density can be due to a variety of processes. As mentioned in paragraph 2.1 above, the present lack of *balance* between fertility and mortality leads to considerable increases in overall population density, particularly in the developing parts of the world. Other reasons comprise *relocation* of large populations. Most migration in the world is from rural to urban areas in the same country, although it also can and does occur between cities and between rural areas, and between countries.

2.3.2 The urbanization process.

Archeological research indicates that the first cities arose along the Tigris and Euphrates rivers between 4000 and 3000 B.C. As pointed out by Davies (1965), no society was urbanized (i.e. a majority of the population living in towns) before 1800 and only one by 1900 (Great Britain). In the *Europe* of 1600, about 1.6 per cent of the population lived in cities with a population of 100,000 or more; by 1700, the figure was about 1.9 per cent and by 1800 about 2.2 per cent. So, on the brink of the Industrial Revolution, Europe was essentially an agrarian continent. In the *United States,* about 6 per cent of the population lived in urban areas in 1800, 15 per cent in 1850, 40 per cent in 1900; today, more than 70 per cent live in cities or in their suburbs. The trend in *Africa* has been similar. Nairobi is growing at an annual rate of 7 per cent, Accra at almost 8 per cent, Kinshasa at 10 per cent and Lusaka (possibly the fastest growing city in Africa if not in the world, cf. United Nations, 1973 b) at 12 per cent.

Toffler (1970) cites data to illustrate that we are now undergoing the most extensive and rapid urbanization the world has ever seen. "In 1850 only four cities on the face of the earth had a population of 1,000,000 or more. By 1900 the number had increased to nineteen. But by 1960, there were 141." According to some forecasts, there will be 275 by the year 2000.

Looking ahead, Steigenga (1964) makes a similar point: "In the year 2,000 the urban population throughout the world will be five time as great as the urban population of 1950. Notwithstanding that the degree of urbanization of Asia is still low, compared with the Western world, the urban population in Asia in 1950 was already five times that of 1900; in Europe, including the Soviet Union, the urban population in 1950 was two and a half times that of 1900." The urban population is presently increasing at a rate of 3.2 per cent per year, but the rates of growth vary in different areas. Maximum growth (5 per cent) is predicted for Africa, and minimum (1.2 per cent) for Europe, cf. table 1. According to recent predictions published by the United Nations (1971 d), total *urban* population at the end of this century will be twice as large as the total *world* population at the beginning of the century.

The very considerable rate of world population growth has been presented and commented upon in paragraph 2.1. It is noteworthy that urban population growth is even more dramatic (figure 8), sometimes being referred to as an *"urban explosion"*. While world population *trebled* in the period 1800–1960, the population living in localities of 20,000 or more inhabitants increased more than *forty times;* the population in localities with 20,000 to 100,000 inhabitants increased almost 35 times and in localities with 100,000 inhabitants or more it increased nearly 40 times (Breese, 1966). When considering such figures, however, it should be remembered that towns and cities move continuously from lower to higher categories, which complicates interpretations.

The growth of urbanization is particularly marked in newly developing countries. As pointed out by the United Nations (1957), "between 1900 and 1950, the population living in cities of 100,000 or more in *Asia* mounted from an estimated 19.4 million to 105.6 million and in *Africa* from 1.4 million to 10.2 million. The same source illustrates that in 1800, 2.4 per cent of the world's population lived in towns compared with more than 30 per cent by 1960. By the turn of the century it is predicted (United Nations, 1971 d) that more than 50 per cent will be found in towns and cities.

A reasonably detailed picture of the average annual rates of growth in urban population over five 10-year periods (1950–2000) is given in table 1. In considering the high African figures it should, however, be kept in mind that the absolute number of Africans living in towns and cities is still relatively low.

Thus, urbanization is moving much faster in the developing countries than it did in the developed countries. In Great Britain, the change from a population with 10 per cent in cities to one with 30 per cent in cities took about 79 years. The same change took 66 years in the U.S., 48 in

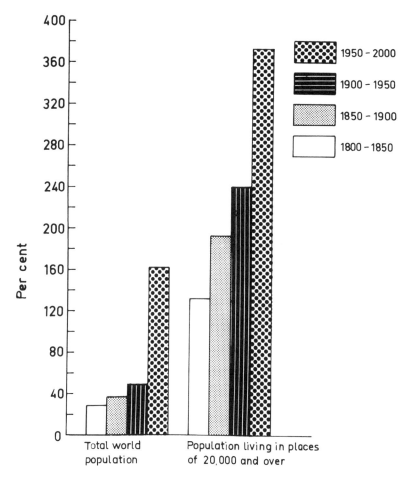

Figure 8. The rate of increase in world and urban population. (Sources: Breese 1966; United Nations 1971 d.)

Germany, 36 in Japan, and 26 in Australia. In the developing countries the change will be even more rapid (Brown, 1972).

In a few generations, then, with practically no time for changes in man's biological equipment – and not even much time for changes in customs – the human environment has undergone a drastic transformation.

2.3.3 The ruralization process.

When considering rural-urban population shifts, political as well as scientific interest has focused almost entirely on urbanization and urban

Table 1. Average annual rates of growth in **urban** *population, 1950–2000, in major regions of the world (per cent).*

Region	1950–60	1960–70	1970–80	1980–90	1990–2000
World total	3.4	3.2	3.2	3.1	2.8
More developed regions	2.9	2.1	1.9	1.7	1.4
Less developed regions	4.3	4.6	4.5	4.2	3.7
East Asia	5.5	4.1	3.8	3.4	2.9
South Asia	3.3	4.4	4.5	4.2	3.6
Europe	1.7	1.7	1.5	1.4	1.2
Soviet Union	4.1	2.7	2.3	2.1	1.7
Africa	4.7	4.7	5.0	5.0	4.7
Northern America	2.7	2.0	1.9	1.8	1.5
Latin America	4.6	4.4	4.2	3.9	3.5
Oceania	2.9	2.5	2.5	2.3	1.8

Source: United Nations (1971 d)

areas. The processes operative in rural areas and their effects on the population have attracted much less attention. In considering these processes it should be noted that the outflux from rural to urban areas, although impressive, does not necessarily reduce the rural population because of the concomitant effects of high fertility and decreasing mortality. But the outflux is often rather selective, primarily comprising healthy young adults, whereas infants, children, old people and handicapped tend to be left behind. Briefly, then, the ruralization process can, but need not, thin out the rural population. However, it usually involves very considerable qualitative changes in the composition of the residual population.

Considering world trends and predictions, as well as trends and

Table 2. Average annual rates of growth or decline in **rural** *population 1950–2000, in major regions of the world (per cent).*

Region	1950–60	1960–70	1970–80	1980–90	1990–2000
World total	1.1	1.4	1.4	1.2	0.8
More developed regions	−0.6	−0.5	−0.8	−0.9	−1.2
Less developed regions	1.6	1.8	1.7	1.5	1.0
East Asia	0.9	1.0	0.7	0.2	−0.3
South Asia	1.9	2.2	2.3	2.0	1.4
Europe	−0.3	−0.5	−0.7	−0.9	−1.0
Soviet Union	−0.1	−0.4	−0.7	−0.9	−1.3
Africa	1.7	1.9	2.2	2.2	1.9
Northern America	0.0	−0.3	−0.4	−0.5	−0.8
Latin America	1.3	1.3	1.0	0.8	0.5
Oceania	1.2	1.3	1.5	1.7	1.5

Source: United Nations (1971 d)

predictions for various regions, we find that world rural population (table 2), is rising by 1.4 per cent a year and probably will continue to increase, from 1,782 millions in 1950 to 3,190 millions in the year 2000. Behind this trend lies a population increase in the *developing* regions that counterbalances a more or less pronounced decrease in the developed countries. This increase is particularly marked in South Asia, where the man-land ratio is already very high. Without a single regional exception, the *developed* countries of the world are reducing their rural population and will most probably continue to do so in the foreseeable future. And even in some of today's developing regions, predictions have been made of a net decrease, albeit a moderate one.

2.4 Migration

The concept of migration is by no means homogeneous. Migration can be intercontinental, intracontinental, internal (i.e. within one country) and local (i.e. within a community). The movements may include short visits, seasonal and other short-period turnovers, attempts to establish an urban residence which may succeed or fail, as well as definitive transfers of residence. Available fragmentary statistics indicate that international movement over great distances has diminished in recent decades, movements over shorter distances have become more frequent, and that population gains by urban places at the expense of the rural community have accelerated most (United Nations, 1971 d).

According to Cook (1957), the amount of people migrating from their homelands to a new area in the period 1946–1955 can be estimated at about 50 millions. If this period is extended to cover the years from 1930 to the present, the amount of migrants may well surpass 70 millions. McKinlay and McKinlay (1972) compare this figure with the amount of people migrating to the United States between 1820 and 1965, which is 43 millions, or with the total number of people migrating from Europe and Asia to North and South America and Oceania during the 19th and early 20th centuries, which was about 60 millions (National Academy of Sciences, 1971).

According to Zwingmann and Pfister-Ammende (1973), more than 100 million people of the northern hemisphere left their homeland or were forcefully separated from it during the first half of the 20th century. They migrated, they were displaced or deported, they fled from persecution. The authors summarize the classification of the motivations for the move as follows:

☐ *physical:* e.g. war or natural calamities like earthquakes, droughts, famine, floods, climate, etc;

☐ *economic:* e.g. underemployment, low material living standards, absence of social security, move ordered by government (flooding of areas related to dam construction) – industrialization and urbanization, advanced social security benefits;

☐ *social:* family trouble, housing and occupational difficulties – future of children, attraction by relatives or friends already moved;

☐ *psychological:* personal conflict, escapism, restlessness, difficulties of adjustment to existing society, fear of persecution or war – transcultural interest, sense of adventure;

☐ *religious:* religious intolerance – religious freedom;

☐ *political:* discrimination, persecution – political ambition;

☐ *professional:* e.g. inadequate pay, inadequate research facilities, etc.

These and other factors make the migrating population a highly selected pick of the total population, with regard to sex, age and social and ethnic background. In some countries of Latin America, for instance, many unmarried young women move to towns, while in some Asian countries the temporary migrants comprise many married men who sooner or later return to their rural families.

A number of those who migrate are repatriates, returning to their home country because they have been released from P.O.W. captivity or because they could not adapt to the country to which they had immigrated. Other subcategories are the millions of foreign workers who have moved to countries or cities offering or just believed to offer better pay and/or work opportunities. According to a report of the International Labour Organization (cf Gould, 1973), "the number of migrant workers and their families in the countries of western Europe is thought to be 11 million and the total number of such workers in seven of these countries is estimated at about 7 million, distributed more or less as follows: Federal Republic of Germany: 2,350,000; Belgium: 220,000; France: 1,700,000; Netherlands: 125,000; Great Britain: 1.560,000; Sweden: 220,000; and Switzerland: 900,000. The pattern of this migration is highly varied as regards ethnic origin, cultural background and language."

In considering migration it must further be noted whether we refer to the movement of migrant workers with very limited skills or the movement of skilled workers and professionals ("brain drain"). The movement of the former usually has a dramatic impact on population growth and often markedly influences their own quality of life as well as the situation of the regions from and to which they move. Although the latter category makes but a numerically modest contribution to migratory currents, this may aggravate the existing imbalances in the availability of intellectual manpower and accordingly can be of considerable economic and social importance.

Part of this migration is within countries (internal migration). In the United States, approximately 20 per cent of the total population moves every year. According to data cited by Toffler (1970), average residence in one place in 70 major United States cities (including New York) is less than 4 years, a period well worth contrasting with the lifelong residence in one place characteristic of yesterday's rural villager. The same author mentions as an illustrative curiosity that of the 885,000 listings in the Washington, D.C., telephone book in 1969, over half were different from the year before.

Briefly, then, migration has already reached very impressive dimensions and will probably continue to increase.

3 The target: high risk groups

3.1 Some general considerations

"One man's meat is another man's poison". This empirical fact obviously reflects differences in man's psychobiological "programming" due to genetic factors and earlier environmental influences. The latter include physical as well as psychosocial stimuli. The complex pattern of "programming" factors makes every individual unique and determines his propensity to react in one way or another, e.g. in response to population density and change. Yet, individuals can be categorized into groups which are characterized by their propensity to react to certain stimuli, qualitatively as well as quantitatively. In consequence, individuals within such groups may exhibit different kinds and/or degrees of response to a given environmental influence. This difference can range all the way from a physically, mentally, or socially disabling reaction in those with the least capacity to withstand stressor exposure, to little more than a transitory irritation or annoyance in the more strongly endowed. As pointed out in a recent WHO report (1973 a), there are, on the other hand, stressful influences of such magnitude that they can overwhelm the individual, whatever his strength, and thus reduce the importance of variations in susceptibility. Accordingly, the agent-host-disease relation can vary depending upon the relative importance of stressor intensity and host vulnerability. Thus, one no longer asks, "How many at risk?" but "How much at risk is each individual?" (Lader, 1971). Some of the determinants of individual susceptibility are age, sex and present illness or state of chronic disability. Similarly, group susceptibility may vary, depending upon group cohesion and group support. In the present context we feel unable to divide humanity into a large number of subgroups, from which predictions could be made in relation to general or specific vulnerability to potentially noxious influences. Only three broad categories will be mentioned in more detail, namely infants and children, old people and the handicapped.

Before discussing these categories it should be mentioned that potentially pathogenic reactions, particularly to psychosocial stimuli, are heavily influenced by the individual's *ability to cope,* which, again, is a function of his psychobiological "program". Facing a threatening situation, some people resort to denial. They "refuse" to perceive a threat

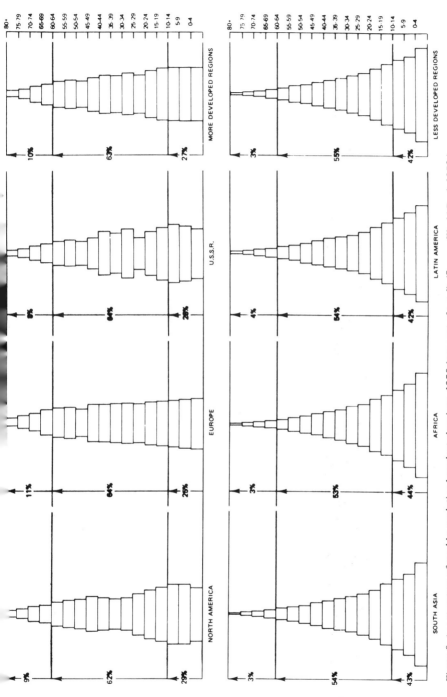

Figure 9. Age structure of world population by selected regions, 1970 (per cent of total). (Source: World Bank 1973.)

39

considered quite obvious by other people. If this psychological defence mechanism is effective, peace of body and mind may be preserved even in the face of what objectively would be considered as dramatic calamities.

Another example of coping mechanisms is intellectualization. Here, the individual or group is trying to calculate the risk in almost statistical terms ("why should this happen to me?"). Others resort to magical or dogmatic thinking, whereas others again make use of "displacement", focusing on trivial risks and stressors, thereby decreasing their awareness of more serious threats. For a far more complete discussion of adaptive and maladaptive coping, see Lazarus (1967).

In paragraph 2.4 we mentioned the many reasons why people migrate. The interaction between such factors and coping and other characteristics of individuals and groups, makes it easy to understand the enormous variability as to outcome in terms of quality of life caused by exposure to objectively similar or even identical population factors and environmental influences.

3.2 Infants and children

As indicated by data presented in Chapter 2, a very considerable proportion of the world population is under 15 years of age. In developing countries, this age group accounts for an estimated 42 per cent of the population (United Nations, 1971 c; World Bank, 1972) and the resultant typical age distribution differs greatly from a highly developed low-fertility country (figure 9). Due to present sharp decreases in infant and child mortality, this will have a dramatic secondary influence on the age distribution of tomorrow, when these children reach reproductive age.

As illustrated in figure 10, the *developing* part of the world contributes the great majority of total world births. This means that very substantial proportions of the population are and will continue to be

☐ under 15 years of age,

☐ living in developing countries, in the majority of cases still under socioeconomic conditions that are highly unsatisfactory.

Thus, increased vulnerablility due to infancy and childhood is often combined with — or even potentiated by — an extremly underprivileged socioeconomic status. In rural areas, some protection is afforded by family and social group cohesion. But if the main provider of the family has to leave the village to work in town, or if the entire nuclear family has moved to an urban area where both parents have to work to maintain

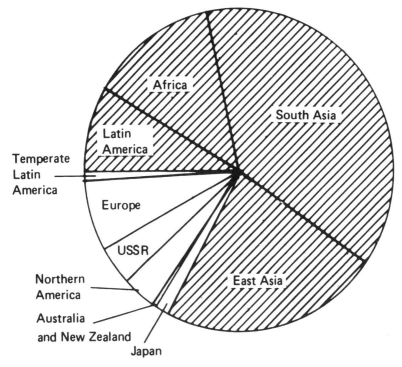

Figure 10. Births in the world: percentage of total by region, 1969. Percentage of world total: South Asia 38.0, East Asia 22.8, Africa 13.2, Latin America 8.7, Europe 7.1, USSR 3.9, Northern America 3.6, Japan 1.6, Temperate Latin America 0.9, Australia and New Zealand 0.3. (Source: United Nations 1971 c.)

the children, with no one left to care for and look after them sufficiently, the result is often bound to be deleterious, because the child easily becomes undernourished and exposed to adverse environmental conditions as soon as it is weaned. As already pointed out, these and other unfavourable influences tend to combine (cf. Levi, 1974).

3.3 Old people

Life expectancy has increased progressively. In the *developed* countries, the average expectation at birth is now 71 years. In the *developing* world, the figures are lower, being over 60 years in Latin America, around 57 years in Asia and only about 47 years in Africa. Even so, the overall trend has meant that the proportion of the entire population over 65 years has increased and is considerable (figure 9). It is well known that high age increases the organism's vulnerability to almost any noxious influence, besides decreasing performance and the ability to cope (cf. Kuhlen, 1967). As in the case of infants and children, old people are at risk for two reasons which often concur. First, old age usually enhances general vulnerability and might be accompanied by an increased incidence of disability in the form of blindness, hearing impairments, paralysis, impairment or absence of extremities, etc (Riley and Foner, 1968). Second, the socioeconomic situation of the great majority of old people is more or less unsatisfactory. Under stable, rural conditions or in highly developed countries, old people are taken care of either by members of their family or by society. Under conditions of rapid urbanization (and ruralization) or under migration, the old are often left behind without young or middle-aged relatives to provide for them, or they find themselves in urban slums where exposure to noxious stimuli is high and protection is low or absent. The increase in mean life expectancy due to improved health care, sanitation and nutrition makes it possible for increasingly large groups of people to reach old age.

Although this adds years to their life, it often does not add much if any life to their years.

3.4 The physically, mentally and socially handicapped

The third group at risk is much more complex and difficult to define. This is due to the fact that a handicap must always be considered in relation to the psychosocial and physical ecosystem in which the individual is expected to function. As the environmental setting varies enormously from community to community, the importance of any single handicap or pattern of handicaps will differ according to the environmental setting and compensatory potentials in the individual. Suffice it to say that litterally *hundreds of millions* of people are severely physically, mentally or socially handicapped. Examples of such groups are the blind, the deaf, the disabled, the mentally retarded or ill, the drug addicts and alcoholics, those belonging to a minority group, or being a migrant or transient. In highly developed countries one may also focus on other, "lesser" social handicaps. In many developing countries this is next to impossible in view of the enormous poverty, the apathy of many of the underpriviledged and the lack of social and medical services.

Briefly, then, the handicapped constitute a high risk group even in highly developed countries. In developing countries they do so to a much greater degree, and their fate depends almost entirely on group cohesion and family support. When such means of support tend to fail, e.g. due to extreme poverty, social disorganization and the dissolution of families by urbanization and migration, the quality of·life of the handicapped will necessarily be close to nil.

Again, the increased vulnerability often coincides with an increased exposure to the most vicious environments. Noise, pollution, overcrowding, nutritional deficiencies and low hygienic standards characterize huge settlement areas not only in the developing countries but in the slums of many developed countries too. To these very areas, various segregational forces "sort out" exactly those individuals who are most in need of a more favourable environment. In this way, maximal vulnerability is combined with maximal exposure to environmental stressors, increasing the risk of a subsequent decline in health and wellbeing.

4 Interacting variables: the environmental setting

4.1 Some general considerations

As pointed out in Chapter 3, population structures and processes are but one of several determinants of the quality of life. Individual and group characteristics are also important for the outcome, as are the characteristics − physical and psychosocial − of the environment in which the population structures and processes are operative. As emphasized in the introductory paragraphs, these and other factors are components in a complex ecosystem with several routes for mutual interaction. This means that, say, rapid population growth may have consequences in terms of urbanization, economic development and social change, but also in terms of, say, environmental pollution, and eventually in terms of various aspects of the quality of life, with every component mutually influencing every other. Clearly, it is impossible within the scope of the present document to sort out the effects of every conceivable or even every important combination of stimuli and interacting variables. But we try in the following to present some of those environmental settings that are known or suspected to be particularly relevant.

4.2 Urban and rural environments

Urban environments are not homogeneous, comprising towns, agglomerations, city regions and urban zones (figure 1). The density of settlements in a town is usually a function of the value of the land for various purposes. The higher the value, the more intense the exploitation. The value of a certain piece of land is influenced among other things by its accessibility in relation to other areas and to natural resources. In fact, the value of land in a city reflects the spatial accessibility as determined by transportation, i.e. the travel, time and costs involved in moving from one point to another. In easily accessible areas of a country with a market economy, land price goes up. Consequently, activities which are economically weak are pushed to cheaper areas in the periphery of the town. In the borderline between the expanding urban nucleus and this periphery, decay zones are created while waiting for expropriation. Industries, offices, workshops and trade take over the residential quarters. The highly *industrialized,* rapidly expanding region is characterized by a rapid influx of people looking for new jobs. Simultaneously, there is an outflux from the central parts, where offices take over (Carlestam and Levi, 1971).

With rising economic standards, ever-increasing space is demanded for housing and places of work. This, in turn, further increases the demand for land, transportation etc. Transportation, in turn, occupies increasing areas of land.

The combined effect of these trends can become an *urban sprawl* – a few nodes of very dense settlement surrounded by housing areas characterized by low exploitation.

In order to maintain the functional capacity of the town, the transportation system is expanded, as are the surrounding marginal prohibited areas. This, in turn, leads in a spiral to further expansion in space, which further increases the demand for transportation etc. This continuous expansion is made possible by the development of transportation technology with an ever-increasing geographical range.

Cities in the *developing* countries also expand. However, they grow much less in space in relation to the size of the population. This is because the settlement density is much higher and the inhabitants are less

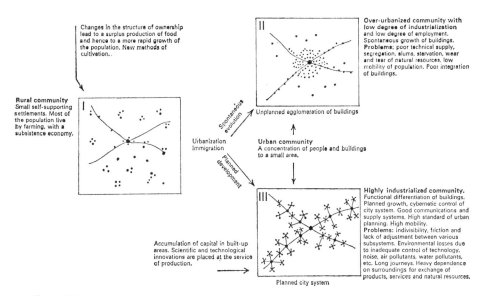

Figure 11. The urbanization process. Two conceivable extreme forms of evolution and their particular problems (both forms, II and III, are based on the same population figures). In practice, urban communities today represent a combination of these two extremes (Carlestam and Levi, 1971).

mobile owing to a lack of transportation systems. Accordingly, these cities already are and increasingly become "overurbanized", with resulting hygienic and social problems, including high unemployment. Thus, there are obvious differences between the urbanization processes and urban environments in industrialized as compared with developing countries. These differences should be kept in mind. Two different developments, representing two extremes, are visualized in figure 11 (Carlestam and Levi, 1971). The environmental problems to which they lead are different. This illustrates the difficulty of formulating general conclusions as to the environmental problems of different cities. Unless the conditions can be specified, general conclusions are usually not valid.

One of the effects of rapid urbanization in developing countries is the creation of huge *squatter settlements*. In most cities of the developing world, slums and squatter settlements account for one third to a half of the population (United Nations World Housing Survey, 1973). The term *"slum"* refers to areas of authorized, usually older, housing which are deteriorating in the sense of being underserviced, overcrowded and dilapidated. The urban *squatters* are the "illegal" occupants of urban land. Unable to obtain a piece of land or shelter as legitimate tenants or home owners within the urban society, they use their own initiative; temporary shelters are set up first on any site where they can enjoy some security of tenure within or on the periphery of the town or city; in time, they can exert a moral claim to the site (Juppenlatz, 1970).

Needless to say, the physical and psychosocial environment of slums and squatters often does not offer even a modicum of the prerequisites for a good life. Accordingly, the frequent existence of such environmental settings is already a definite threat to the quality of life today, and particularly so in the developing countries. In addition, the situation is being aggravated by the fact that in these countries, slums and squatter settlements are by far the fastest growing parts of urban areas.

A current UNICEF report entitled "Children and adolescents in slums and shanty towns in developing countries" (E/ICEF/L.1277 and Add. 1) expresses the arithmetic of "transitional" settlement growth as follows:

Natural increase, in *modern* sector . . . . 2 per cent of city population
Natural increase, in *slum* sector . . . . 1 per cent of city population
Rural-urban *migration to slums* . . . . 3 per cent of city population

Total city growth . . . . 6 per cent

Since slums with one third of the city population account for the city growing at a rate of 4 per cent, they themselves are growing at a rate of 12 per cent.

What has been said above has obvious implications for the *macro* aspect of the characteristics and effects of urban conglomerates, i.e. at community level. In addition, one ought to consider the *micro* aspect, comprising man's most immediate environment, i.e. at individual level. Both include the combination of e.g. housing, transport, water supply and waste disposal.

When discussing urbanization and urban life, the importance of these influences is often emphasized at the expense of those of ruralization and rural life. This is partly due to a propensity to imagine the countryside as an idyllic spot in the sense of Jean Jacques Rousseau, forgetting the often extreme backwardness and poverty of rural areas. At the United Nations' Symposium in Stockholm on Population, Resources and Environment (1973) it was empasized that however bad the situation might be in the cities, "it is unlikely that large scale migration (to urban areas) would be occurring if conditions were not still worse in the countryside".

Thus, whilst Ward and Dubos (1972), believe that "the first need is to take the strain off existing cities", and Bose (1973) argues that "the first need is to take the strain off rural areas – the strain of poverty, unemployment and economic and social stagnation" it would seem desirable to do something about cities and rural areas simultaneously. In 1970, 72 per cent of the world's population lived in rural areas. In the same year, some 82 per cent of all rural inhabitants lived in developing countries, often under very miserable conditions. Accordingly there is reason to agree with Bose (1973), who argues that more attention should be paid to problems of rural environment: "Otherwise the talk of quality of life would refer only to the elite and not to the masses".

4.3 Industrialism

Perhaps the most logical way to begin this part of the review is by examining the nature of industrialism (cf. Slotkin, 1960). This constitutes a set of interdependent customs – what anthropologists call a trait complex – characterized by the use of complex technological equipment which can neither be owned nor operated by a single person, extensive division of labour, formal industrial organization, and the interdependence of the industrial organization and a wider society. One or more of these characteristics may be found in other productive systems, and particularly in manufacture (taken in its literal sense). But in none of them are these characteristics developed to such a high degree, producing qualities unique to industrialism.

Viewed in a historical perspective, the process of industrialization was closely linked to organizational changes in agriculture, especially to a change in ownership leading to larger units, which, in turn, facilitated the introduction of new methods of cultivation. This change yielded increased food production and, secondarily, more rapid population growth. The combination of these effects constituted a basis for the subsequent process of industrialization (Carlestam and Levi, 1971).

Industrialization also stimulated the development of transportation, which, in turn, created — and made possible — large markets for products from a mass manufacturing that became increasingly specialized. The cities no longer had to rely exclusively upon the nearby farming districts to maintain their growing population. One of the revolutionary changes was that possibilities were created of transporting relatively cheap but bulky articles to new and larger markets, because transportation costs decreased.

Industrialization started at the end of the 18th century in England, in Sweden about a century later. Although the process started rather late in Sweden compared with other West European countries, it has since developed rather fast, leading to various forms of imbalance, e.g. between the supply of and demand for job opportunities, housing, and natural resources. Basically, these problems in Sweden are of the same type as in other highly industrialized countries.

One of the concomitants of industrialization comprises structural changes in technology and economy, leading inter alia to scale and magnitude changes in the physical environment. The mesh widths of the transportation net increase, and various facilities are concentrated into rather few but large groups. Simultaneously, each piece of land becomes increasingly specialized, serving only one exclusive function, e.g. living, working, travelling or recreation (cf. Carlestam and Levi, 1971).

This specialization automatically creates problems, especially for children, the aged and the handicapped, because their fields of activity tend to be restricted. Consequently, many individuals are compelled to live in an environment that is incomplete. Admittedly, attempts have been made to compensate for this by providing the missing environmental elements, e.g. some type of service, or else the individuals have been given opportunities to increase their mobility, e.g. by vehicles for conveying children to school, cars adapted for disabled persons etc.

Industrialization and technological development involve rapid wear and tear of natural and man-made environments as well as diminution of natural resources. Technological development also leads to rapid changes in social institutions (cf Adler-Karlsson, 1973 and 1974). In considering the effects of industrialization, it tends to be forgotten that this process is by no means confined to the developing countries. Both these and the developed world are undergoing pronounced technological and social change, impressive not only in its magnitude but also through its suddenness.

Of paramount importance is the rapid development of *mass communications,* both through travel and through mass media. This technology brings the starving African village right into the living rooms of affluent societies. But is also informs the starving, overcrowded populations in the developing world about the enormous inequality in access to various determinants of levels of living.

Another consequence of industrialization and technological development seems to be an impressive increase in *noise* exposure. Noise has been defined as any unwanted sound and named by some as the most prevalent "waste product" of our age. Numerous authors have shown that noise provokes physiological stress reactions, not only as concomitants to the distress reactions implicit in the very definition of noise, but also through reflex stimulation of the auditory nerves and on to the hypothalamic-hypophyseal system (cf. Carlestam et al., 1974).

It may well be that in the dawn of the history, noise tended to be a signal of danger or else a characteristic of a situation requiring muscular work. In order to cope optimally with a challenging environment or even to survive, the human organism had to prepare for action, inter alia by the non-specific adaptive reaction pattern defined as stress.

More often than not, the meaning of noise in today's societies is completely different from in the Stone Age. Yet, and according to one hypothesis, our genetically determined psychobiological programming still makes us react as though muscular activity were an adequate reaction to any sudden, unexpected or annoying noise stimulus, i.e. in a non-adaptive or even maladaptive manner.

4.4 Economic factors

Population growth has profound economic effects, which in turn react on population growth. Their complex interaction has profound repercussions on the quality of life. Briefly, then, economic factors can be causes as well as effects of population growth.

A crude measure of material living standards in different nations is furnished by the *gross national product* (GNP), plus its distribution among countries and among individuals within countries. Although this measure has been much criticized, and for good reasons, it is the most universally utilized. Whatever measure we prefer to choose, there is no doubt concerning two basic facts: (1) there exists an enormous economic

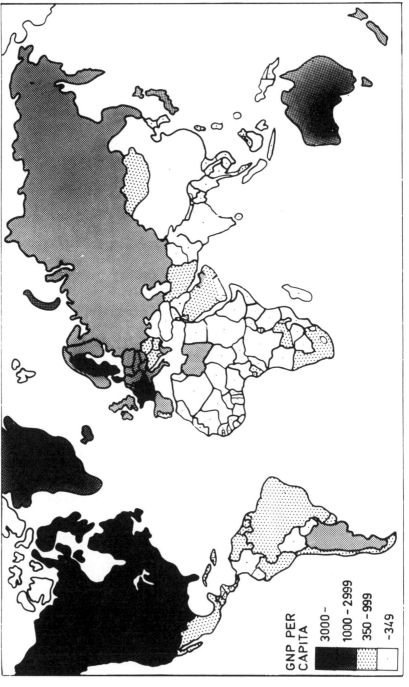

GNP PER
CAPITA

3000 –

1000 – 2999

350 – 999

– 349

Output per person
US$ 1960 prices

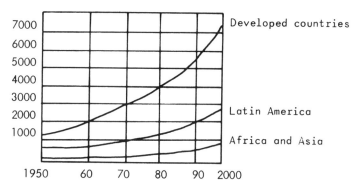

Figure 13. An estimate of the size of the present and future economic gaps between developed and developing countries. (Source: Adler–Karlsson 1973.)

gap between the developed and developing nations, cf figure 12, and (2) this economic gap is continuously widening, partly because of the population explosion in the poor countries (Adler–Karlsson, 1973 and 1974). The present magnitude of this gap is shown in figure 13, and the present GNP change in figure 14.

Although statistics do not bleed, it is easy to imagine what an environment characterized by a GNP of, say, US $ 100 per capita can mean in terms of material prerequisites for even a modicum of quality of life. With some minor exceptions, GNP admittedly tends to rise in the great majority of *developing* countries but so does the population and, accordingly, the pressure on available resources. In addition, the low initial GNP levels should be taken into account when evaluating the percentage GNP increases. In *absolute* terms, these increases are of course still rather low in spite of rather impressive percentages. This is not so in the *developed* countries (cf. Adler–Karlsson, 1973 and 1974).

The increasing public awareness of this economic gap and of related phenomena belongs, however, to the psychosocial aspects of the quality of life and will accordingly be dealt with in Chapter 5. It may well be that the relationship between individual economic resources on the one hand, and aspects of quality of life, on the other, is U-shaped (cf. Kagan and Levi, 1974). Should this be so, extreme poverty as well as extreme affluence would have noxious effects. Clearly, today's problems are much more related to deprivation than to excess. There is probably a threshold, below which the quality of life is low, whatever the measure. On the other hand, above another threshold, an additional increase in

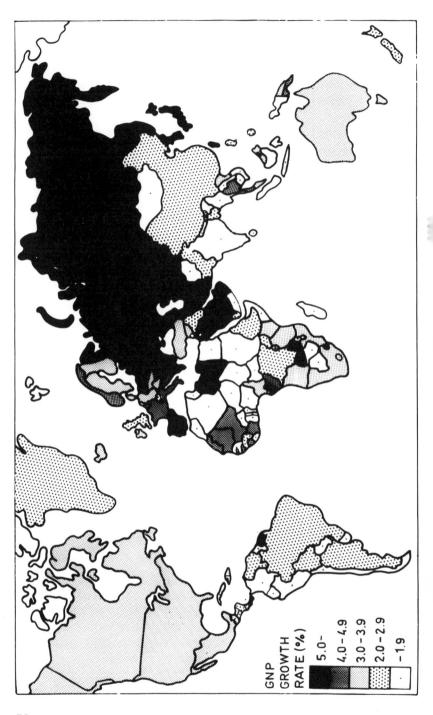

GNP
GROWTH
RATE (%)

5.0–

4.0 – 4.9

3.0 – 3.9

2.0 – 2.9

– 1.9

52

economic levels or even in the resulting "level of living" will by no means result automatically in an increase in the quality of life. The corollary of this might be that excess should be used to make up for deficiency. However, a rational solution requires not only a change in attitude on the part of the people of the developed countries but also a deep understanding of the process involved. Taking from the "rich" to help the "poor" may provide an immediate redress but alone will not perpetuate the correct balance. Also, preoccupation with the goal of an ever increasing GNP detracts from the objective of an ever increasing quality of life.

4.5 Employment

As implied on almost every page of this report, poverty is one of the common denominators of most negative environmental influences, either as a cause of such influences, or as their effect, or as a cause of man's inability to modify their effect. Employment is by far the most important of all possible instruments in our attempt to decrease or eliminate poverty.

Again, today's situation is very far from satisfactory. Unparalleled levels of unemployment exist, particularly in developing countries, due in part to the combined effects of population growth and the introduction of technologies unsuited to local conditions.

Future trends are no less serious. As pointed out in a recent report (United Nations, 1971 c), "by 1975–1980 the annual net increase in the working-age population in the developing countries will have nearly doubled". Before the end of the century it will be three times the rate of increase which prevailed in 1960–1965. With a steady trend towards increasing mechanization (and automation) in industry and even in agriculture, the gainful employment of such enormous populations each year will pose most serious problems. This is so partly because of the present age distribution illustrated by the shape of the population pyramid (cf. figure 9), with a very considerable proportion at present under 15 years of age, i.e. the young people who will be entering the labour force and seeking employment during the next 15 years are already born. In addition, due to improved health, the length of working life may well be extended. A further factor of increasing importance will be the growing participation of women in occupational activities outside the home, a trend generally regarded as almost a prerequisite for a future decline in world fertility.

As a result of these and other trends, the need to provide employment opportunities will rise sharply. *New* job opportunities will have to be created for almost half of these cohorts; after 1980 this will be true of about two third of all the jobs required for newcomers to the labour market. Within the next three decades, there will be more than *one billion new workers* in the developing world (United Nations, 1971 c). This enormous increase can be seen as a threat, or as a challange and an opportunity. Properly handled, it can provide scope for accelerated economic and social development. Otherwise it may well lead to chaos and human suffering.

Employment is a means for material acquisition. But it is also an end in its own right, a way to fulfil psychosocial needs. In many cultures all over the world, gainful employment is the main instrument for self-realization and self-fulfilment. Being deprived of this human right has obvious repercussions on the quality of life.

4.6 Family - related cultural and social factors

Cultural and social factors interact with population variables in an extremely complex way. A few examples are given below.

Particularly in many developing countries, the family organization is a corporate kinship or *extended family system,* in which numerous children are valued as contributing to the strength of the group (United Nations, 1971 c). Some authors refer to these cultural patterns primarily as *social attitudes.* Others point out that they represent the hard facts of life, favouring individual and family group survival. This situation has probably prevailed since the dawn of history. Such a social and cultural system favours high fertility levels. It also contributes, up to a point, to the coping with hardships created by high population growth, through interdependence with children, including production, consumption, leisure activities and assistance during illness and old age.

The authority practiced by the female and/or male leader of each extended family or social group puts decisions concerning family limitation in the hands of these elders, who often resist social change. Many cultures promote early marriage. In others, fatalism tends to characterize the attitude to life. Both may influence population variables and the quality of life (cf. United Nations, 1971 c).

In contrast, most developed countries provide *non-familial* institutions to take care of the young, the old and the handicapped. In such countries, additional children are often regarded as an economic disadvantage and burden. Due to lengthy schooling and legislation against the employment of children, the child is not expected and is really unable to contribute to the economy of the family. Due to inadequate day care facilities in many countries, combined with a cultural pressure on and a need for and by women to work outside the home, the birth of new children is often regarded as a drag on female equality and freedom of choice. It is easy to see that such factors heavily influence reproductive and related behaviour, and, consequently, the quality of life of the entire group.

Cultural factors also influence family attitudes toward various measures of birth control. Examples of such effects are the spotting and bleeding occasionally caused by intrauterine devices (IUD), which may render the woman ritually unclean and unfit for handling food and for intercourse in many Hindu and Moslem communities. Roman Catholic dogma, empasizing procreation of the species as the main function of coitus, counteracts contraceptives as sinful. The rhythm method and abstinence are proposed instead but both are relatively ineffective and can in addition be considered to violate the male prerogatives common, in particular, in some Latin, Roman Catholic cultures (United Nations, 1971 c).

Matters are further complicated by prejudice, superstition and fears surrounding the use of contraceptives. According to some cultures, both contraception and abortion interrupt that which is natural (cf. United Nations, 1971 c).

Although most national family planning programs in developing countries have emphasized female methods of contraception, females have little voice in matters of control over the reproductive process. The level of female education is often low, and husbands are often very reluctant to accord anything like sexual freedom to women (cf. United Nations, 1971 c).

Even where family limitation is propagated, three to four surviving children is often regarded as an ideal or desired family size. Such limitation would go nowhere towards solving problems of population increase (cf. United Nations, 1971 c).

Briefly, then, cultural and social norms counteract several aspects of family planning. In addition, several cultures accord an authoritative, powerful social position to male members who promote the size of the clan as well as to prolific women, while barren women are repudiated and ridiculed (United Nations, 1971 c).

Family-related cultural and social factors also interact with the industrialization process. Goode (1963) points out that "when industrialization takes place, a strong movement toward a conjugal type of family also occurs, its main characteristics being the following:

□ the extended or joint family pattern becomes rare, and corporate kin structures disappear;

☐ a relatively free choice of spouse is possible, based on love, and an independent houshold is set up;

☐ dowry and bride price disappear;

☐ marriages between kin become less common;

☐ authority of the parent over the child, and of husband over the wife, diminishes;

☐ equality between the sexes is greater; the legal system moves toward equality of inheritance among all children".

These processes and effects might, in turn, have powerful influences on various aspects of quality of life.

4.7 Nutrition

The effects of rapid population growth and major rural-urban and other population redistributions depend to a high degree on the food supply of the regions concerned and on its growth. According to FAO (1973), in the 1950's, world food production increased at an annual rate of 3.2 per cent against a population growth of just under 2 per cent, see table 3. In the following decade, the growth of food production fell off significantly in all regions except Latin America. Despite this and continued population growth, food output stayed ahead, although the margin narrowed appreciably. In considering these figures it should be kept in mind, however, that the situation has been and still is one of under- or malnutrition for large populations.

Out of 106 countries for which detailed information is available for the

Table 3. Average annual rate of growth of population and food production (per cent per year).

Region	1952–1960			1960–1970		
	Popula-tion	Food production		Popula-tion	Food production	
		Total	Per capita		Total	Per capita
Africa	2.2	2.8	0.6	2.5	2.6	0.1
Asia	2.0	3.4	1.4	2.2	2.7	0.5
Latin America	2.8	3.2	0.4	2.9	3.5	0.6
USA, Canada, Europe & Oceania	1.3	3.2	1.9	1.1	2.6	1.5
World	1.8	3.2	1.4	2.0	2.8	0.8

Source: FAO (1973)

Table 4. Calorie supply per capita as percentage of established standards, by major regions and selected countries, 1959/61 and 1970.

Region and country	1959/61	1970
Developed Regions		
Japan	100	112
Southern Europe	110	115
Eastern Europe and U.S.S.R.	113	116
Western Europe	115	117
United States and Canada	117	118
Australia and New Zealand	123	122
Developing regions		
Central America	91	92
Costa Rica	95	98
Dominican Republic	82	85
Mexico	105	108
South America	90	96
Argentina and Uruguay	119	119
Brazil	108	114
Peru	82	90
Centrally Planned Asia	76	86
East Asia	91	96
Philippines	85	94
South Asia	92	97
India	85	88
Middle East	96	99
Iran	87	90
North Africa	94	99
Egypt	98	99
East Africa	98	102
Kenya	97	104
West and Central Africa	103	105
Ivory Coast	101	105
Nigeria	102	105

Source: World Bank (1973)

period 1952–1971, population growth outpaced food production in 27; in the more recent period the figure is still larger (FAO, 1973). As a result, food cuts into scarce foreign exchange resources that are badly needed to finance capital investment.

It should further be kept in mind that global, regional or even national means, even when calculated per capita, gloss over the pronouncedly *unequal distribution* within each group and area.

The FAO report further points out that since population growth cannot be matched by a similar expansion of the land under cultivation, the number of persons to be fed per hectare of cultivated land will increase from levels that are already high in countries such as India and China. In countries where land is abundant, new land can perhaps be brought under cultivation, but only after very considerable investments. The remaining alternative is a further increase in crop yields.

A comparison of calorie and protein intakes with nutritional requirements (tables 4 and 5) region by region shows that all sub-regions of Asia, with the exception of Japan and Israel, have deficits in calories, and, that this also applies to Africa excepting Eastern Africa and South Africa, whereas Latin America seems better able to meet calorie requirement. However, as already emphasized, such calculations conceal pronounced inequalities in the distribution of resources, rural-urban differences, etc. The picture is further complicated by pronounced short-term fluctuations in food production due to seasonal and climatic conditions, causing food shortages in regions where the supply is normally adequate. Again, under- or malnutrition is largely a function of poverty. Consequently, considerable proportions may be under- or malnourished in spite of satisfactory mean national calorie per capita availability. Briefly, at least 20 per cent of the population in the less

Table 5 Net protein supply per capita, by selected countries.

Country	No. of grams per day [1]	
	Animal protein	Total
Developed Countries		
Japan	30	75
Portugal	35	82
Germany	55	83
United Kingdom	53	87
U.S.S.R.	36	92
United States and Canada	67	96
France	64	103
Australia and New Zealand	71	106
Developing Countries		
India	6	49
Malaysia (Mainland)	15	49
Dominican Rep.	21	50
Philippines	20	53
Iran	12	55
Ivory Coast	13	59
Costa Rica	27	62
Tunisia	11	63
Mexico	14	66
Brazil	21	67
Kenya	16	68
Turkey	15	78
Argentina	62	105

[1] 1966 or later.
Source: World Bank (1973).

developed areas was undernourished in the not too distant past (FAO, 1963). Recent data (FAO, 1972) indicate that although this percentage may have fallen slightly, the absolute numbers affected will be *at least* of the same order, i.e. some 3–500 million. For reasons reviewed above, this may well represent a gross underestimation of the real incidence.

It may be tempting to cope with this information by resorting to what has been called "the psychological defence of the expert", namely intellectualization. 3–500 million is an enormous figure, difficult for the human mind to translate into terms of human suffering. This is, however, exactly what we should attempt, because the situation under discussion affects 3–500 million individual human beings and their chances of obtaining at least a minimum of basic needs. An even greater number are affected by lack of access to clean drinking water. It has been estimated that this is so for no less than half the total world population!

4.8 The physical environment

As already repeatedly emphasized, the final outcome in terms of quality of life in response to population factors is multifactorial. One of the most easily identifiable aspects of the total environment is its physical component, some of the most important factors of which are climatic, geographical, geological and hydrological. The action of these factors can be modified to a great extent in highly developed countries. In the developing countries, on the other hand, such factors compound with poor sanitary conditions and the accompanying communicable diseases.

Dry heat in deserts, or humid heat in equatorial areas, are examples of factors influencing the quality of life, besides imposing limitations on work ability.

Similarly, cold climates increase morbidity from diseases of the respiratory tract and, when associated with humidity, rheumatic processes. Seasonal variations seem to play a part in the precipitation of certain mental diseases and psychosomatic disorders.

In more industrialized countries, physical and climatic pollution is of great importance for the health and wellbeing of the populations concerned. For a review, the reader is referred to WHO (1972) and to the report of the United Nations' Symposium in Stockholm (1973) on Population, Resources and Environment.

4.9 Environmental factors: some concluding remarks

This brief, oversimplified account of environmental factors relating to population and quality of life demonstrates the close interconnectedness of the main variables. If one variable is influenced, effects will be noted in each of the others. Consequently, it is probably impossible to cope with current and future situations without heeding not just one or two of the components of the total ecosystem, but every major component. This must be done, not in the abstract but for specific regions and under specific circumstances, taking into account not only the natural limits to growth within a finite space but also man-made barriers of an institutional, political and international nature. The unequal distribution of income and power in the world provides examples of such barriers (cf. Adler–Karlsson, 1973 and 1974).

True, we are confronted by an equation with many unknowns. Things are further complicated by the effects being subject to a considerable time lag. We do not know the actual magnitude of ultimately available energy reserves or of new land that can be made available for agriculture. Great ignorance prevails as to the extent to which additional fresh water supplies can be developed or the technological advances that can be made in this and other respects. Neither do we know which disruptions to expect to ecosystems, and the influence of such disruptions, if any, on individual and group behaviour. But although we cannot define and quantify the effects and prospects for each factor separately, still less their complex interactions, we must not fool ourselves by denying that the problem exists. A great many symptoms of the disease are there, even if considerable ignorance still prevails with regard to its causes and the mechanisms for its development.

There is a strong probability that the solution to the problems under discussion can never be found by simplistic strategies, but by combining a number of complementary strategies. The situation is clearly unprecedented in the history of mankind and may well require not only technological but also or even mainly *social innovations,* i.e. the definition of new societal goals and means.

5 The outcome in terms of quality of life

5.1 Level of living

The effects of levels of and changes in various population and environmental variables have been evaluated almost invariably – and often exclusively – in terms of economic parameters. During the last few decades, however, attention has also focused on various aspects of the level of living. According to United Nations (1961), the concept of *level of living* comprises the following nine components:

1. Health
2. Food consumption
3. Education
4. Occupation, work conditions
5. Housing conditions
6. Social security
7. Clothing
8. Recreation, leisure time
9. Human rights

A modified Swedish version (Johansson, 1973) incorporates six of these components but has changed the other three, the new list being as follows:

1. Work and working conditions
2. Economic resources
3. Political resources
4. Schooling
5. Health and the use of medical care
6. Family origin and family relations (social resources)
7. Housing
8. Nutrition
9. Leisure time and pursuits.

According to Johansson (1973), the chief characteristic of the level of living concept is that it both directs and restricts information to the areas where the *political mechanism* serves, by som degree of consensus, to influence living conditions through social policy, and organizes the information into level of living components.

One of the assumptions is that separate indicators of each component should be assigned relative weights through the *political* process, thereby rejecting a unitary measure of welfare, a general welfare product (GWP). A second characteristic is the focus on the individual's *command* over various resources rather than on individual *need satisfaction.* To balance the status quo and elitist bias from the first two characteristics, a third characteristic is added, under the heading political resources. A fourth characteristic is the piecemeal nature of the concept, in contrast to the so-called utopian or unifying approach. This means that the various sub-components should be identified and dealt with one by one.

In their discussion on "Economic Growth — Quantitative and Qualitative Objectives for the 1970s", at the meeting of the OECD Council at Ministerial Level in May, 1970, Ministers stressed that "growth is not an end in itself, but rather an instrument for creating better conditions of life" and that "increased attention must be given to the qualitative aspects of growth, and to the formulation of policies with respect to the broad economic and social choices involved in the allocation of growing resources".

The subsequent programme of work of the OECD has indicated that one important initiative towards that end would be to explore the possibility of developing a set of *social indicators* with the general objectives of:

☐ identifying the social demands, aspirations and problems which are or will likely become major concerns of socio-economic planning processes;

☐ measuring and reporting change relative to these concerns; thus

☐ helping to focus and enlighten public and governmental decision-making.

Phase I of this programme was published recently (OECD, 1973), specifying eight major "goal areas"

A. Health
B. Individual development through learning
C. Employment and quality of working life
D. Time and leisure
E. Command over goods and services
F. Physical environment
G. Personal safety and the administration of justice
H. Social opportunity and participation

Within these main areas, *24 "fundamental social concerns"* have been defined for monitoring welfare development. These indicators comprise:

A. Health

1. The probability of a healthy life through all stages of the life cycle.
2. The impact of health impairments on individuals.

B. Individual development through learning

3. The acquisition by children of the basic knowledge, skills and values necessary for their individual development and their successful functioning as citizens in their society.
4. The availability of opportunities for continuing selfdevelopment and the propensity of individuals to use them.

5. The maintenance and development by individuals of the knowledge, skills and flexibility required to fulfil their economic potential and to enable them to integrate themselves in the economic process if they wish to do so.
6. The individual's satisfaction with the process of individual development through learning, while he is in the process.
7. The maintenance and development of the cultural heritage relative to its positive contribution to the well-being of the members of various social groups.

C. Employment and quality of working life

8. The availability of gainful employment for those who desire it.
9. The quality of working life.
10. Individual satisfaction with the experience of working life.

D. Time and leisure

11. The availability of effective choices for the use of time.

E. Command over goods and services

12. The personal command over goods and services.
13. The number of individuals experiencing material deprivation.
14. The extent of equity in the distribution of command over goods and services.
15. The quality, range of choice and accessibility of private and public goods and services.
16. The protection of individuals and families against economic hazards.

F. Physical environment

17. Housing conditions.
18. Population exposure to harmful and/or unpleasant pollutants.
19. The benefit derived by the population from the use and management of the environment.

G. Personal safety and the administration of justice

20. Violence, victimization and harassment suffered by individua.
21. Fairness and humanity in the administration of justice.
22. The extent of confidence in the administration of justice.

H. Social opportunity and participation

23. The degree of social inequality.
24. The extent of opportunity for participation in community life, institutions and decision-making.

5.2 Quality of life

Perusing these 24 indicators and a number of "sub-concerns" not listed in our review, one finds that although some compromise the *individual's own* evaluation of his situation, the majority do not. Although not stated explicitly, the headings suggest that most of the evaluations are expected to be made by experts and other authorities, with little room for feedback from the grassroot level of the population.

This is not to say that the latter type of indicators are less important. Obviously they constitute major social concerns. But our point is that they need an essential subjective complement, as indicated in our introductory chapter (p. 12). This complement would enable us to introduce the concept of *"quality of life" as experienced by each individual and by each group.* Although this concept is no doubt heavily dependent in many respects on objective situational characteristics comprised in the level of living concept, there is certainly no one-to-one relationship.

An objectively high level, or even an increase in, say, economic resources, housing or leisure time can – but need not necessarily – be accompanied by a high level or an increase in individual satisfaction, well-being and quality of life. The main reason for such a possible seemingly paradoxical lack of concordance is that – above a certain modicum of level of living – the major determinant of individual quality of life is the *"fit"*, or *"matching"* between situational characteristics (demands and opportunities) and the individual's expectations, abilities and needs *as perceived by the individual himself.*

Against this background we argue that *the "level of living" we refer to is an instrument, not an end in itself.*

This instrument can and must be used to attain the highest possible quality of life for each individual and each group but is just one of several determinants. Further, such attempts must always be supplemented with continuous "subjective" feedback from all those concerned into the political decision making process. Such an "ecological" model for social and economic policy (including population and environmental policy) should further − by definition − take into account the *totality* of all components concerned, balancing against each other the various needs of the individual, and the politically determined priorities concerning the needs of various individuals and groups.

We might well eventually end up with some kind of "Gross National Welfare Product" or "Gross National Satisfaction Product", almost identical with the widely used "health" concept originally proposed by the founding fathers of the World Health Organization: "not only the absence of infirmity or disease but also a state of physical and mental and social wellbeing" (The Preparatory Committee of the International Health Conference, ECOSOC, E/H/PC/W/2, 21 March 1946), cf. page 13.

Within this quality of life framework we intend to discuss what is known and suspected with regard to the effects of population variables on high risk and other groups as modified by various components of the environmental setting. Although we would have liked to apply the principle of man-environment fit throughout our discourse, using quality of life as our criterion, this could not be done for the simple reason that few of the studies reviewed by us present information in this form.

We clearly recognize the close interconnectedness of all variables and their continuous feedback in the complex ecosystem comprising total man in his total environment, although we still feel unable to gather the entire process into a single formula, however complex.

5.3 Rapid social change

A common denominator of most population variables discussed in this document is the element of rapid or even accelerating change. This applies to migration, urbanization, ruralization, and increase and decrease in population density. A high population density further represents a high potential for many and rapid environmental changes due to recurrent encounters with a great number of other people, many of them strangers to each other competing for limited resources. According to this viewpoint, many elements inherent in these situations may produce overstimulation, cf. the right part of the inverted U-shaped curve (figure 3, page 19). Rural life, particularly if stagnant and devoid of vitality, may produce the opposite stimulation extreme, namely understimulation, cf. the left part of the curve. According to our hypothesis, *both* extremes might be deleterious to human wellbeing.

In particular, the environment characterized by rapid, accelerating, marked and numerous changes exposes individuals and groups to ever-increasing adaptional demands. It has been hypothesized (Fröberg and Levi, 1971; Froberg et al., 1971; Levi, 1972 a) that every environmental change constitutes a stressor, which can trigger off the phylogenetically old adaption pattern ("stress") originally preparing the organism for fight and flight or other types of physical activity to promote survival of the individual and the species. This reaction pattern is mobilized in response not only to actual environmental changes, to over- and understimulation, but also to threats of such events or generally to any open-ended situation (for reviews, see Levi, 1971 a and 1972 a). It is assumed that this process is closely related to the rate of wear and tear in the organism (cf. Selye, 1971; Levi, 1972 a).

As mentioned on page 22, a number of studies have demonstrated a significant, positive statistical correlation between the degree of "life change" to which an individual has been exposed (e.g. the "life changes" usually associated with urbanization) and subsequent "health changes" as reflected in morbidity in various diseases.

5.4 Migration and upprooting

The stimuli evoked by migration, urbanization and urban life, and by high and/or increasing population density are often closely related, partly because urbanization implies migration and subsequent exposure to urban life as well as to high and/or increasing population density. But there are also differences between the processes; therefore they will be discussed under separate headings, although some overlapping cannot be avoided.

Let us first consider *migration.* Kjellström (personal communication) discusses the migration process in terms of a number of *stress-producing* elements. Decreased possibilities of earning a living in a certain area can lead to stress. The resultant situation obliges the individual to decide whether or not to migrate and the decision-making process may likewise involve stress. The result of such a decision may be either migration, which might produce stress, or a decision to stay, which again can be stress-producing. Arrival in the new environment can mean exposure to adaptional demands, which may provoke stress. Accordingly, the stressors in connection with migration, particularly when this is involuntary, can involve (a) lack of maintenance because of lack of job, (b) insecurity in connection with the decision making process, (c) demands to enter a new job, with or without previous training. (d) departure from an environment to which one was accustomed, (e) adaptation to a new environment and new social contacts etc. Those remaining in what is often an increasingly ruralized area face a continuous decline in population and/or a change in its composition. This may mean living with an increasing proportion of elderly people, being exposed to a shortage of job opportunities, and to decay in municipal economy, resulting in gradual deterioration of public and private services.

Further, and most important, in response to migration, the traditional *extended family tends to dissolve* (Sangsingkeo, 1964). The migrants to the great urban conglomerations are for the most part young men who have to adapt swiftly to city life, for which they often are unequipped. They may maintain some contact with their families in the rural areas for a time, but the influence of the patriarchal head, the tribal chief or senior members of the family may decline, and there may be no other factor controlling conduct to take its place. Thus, *values* and *patterns of behaviour* may be threatened. Meanwhile, this drain of the young men to cities leaves certain rural areas mostly with women and old people. The break-up of family ties may result in a decline in intra-group protection and support. Productivity and quality of life there may sink to low levels.

Since the first studies by Ödegaard (1932) and Malzberg (1940), much attention has been paid to the possible association between migration and *mental health*. The three principal hypotheses concerning the interrelationships (Murphy, 1965) are:

☐ certain mental disorders incite their victims to migrate;

☐ the process of migration creates mental strain which, in turn, precipitates mental disorder in susceptible individuals;

☐ there is a non-essential association between migration and certain other predisposing or precipitating factors, such as age, social class, and culture conflict.

The relationships which have been found are rather inconsistent and diverse, probably because all three hypotheses describe only part of them, and to an extent which varies from one investigation to another. Furthermore, the great majority of studies are retrospective and have not allowed for the *motives* for migration, the migrants' aspirations and *expectations,* their social relationships and whether they moved singly or in groups. Does their migration result in uprooting? Do they migrate to more favourable − or worse − environmental conditions? Are they forced to leave because of prosecution or destitution or do they respond to a marginal increase offered to someone who was already quite affluent?

As pointed out by Kantor in her recent review (personal communication), studies by Malzberg (1936 a, 1936 b), Malzberg and Lee (1956), Locke et al. (1960), and Lazarus et al. (1963) indicate a positive association between interstate migration and ill health; interstate migrants were generally found to have higher rates of mental illness than non-migrants.

Studies in which this was *not* the case include those of Jaco (1960) and Kleiner and Parker (1959, 1965). Jaco (1960) found that rates of mental illness were not significantly higher for migrants to Texas than for natives of that state. Since Jaco distinguished between "transients" and "migrants" and used data only for "migrants", his findings point to the *type* of migration or transiency as a possible intervening variable. Intervening psychosocial variables, such as social status, status consistency, and the discrepancy between one's achievement and level of aspiration, might explain some of the confusing results; cf. also Dalgard (1972).

An interesting illustration of the relationship between migration, possible change in life-style and morbidity has been furnished by Wolf (1971). The study focused on the little town of Roseto, Pennsylvania, founded by immigrants from southern Italy. In spite of the migration, they have kept this village as something of a South Italian island among the Anglo-Saxon population. The preserved strong family ties and pronounced unity and mutual support of the Roseto villagers, and their patriarchal family life, together with great respect for elders, made their pattern of life similar to a South Italian one and very different from the social pattern of the neighbouring, more Americanized societies. In spite of their otherwise similar way of life and genetic background, the Roseto population had a markedly lower risk of illness or death due to heart infarction during early life. Similarly, Italian workers in Switzerland and Yemenite Jews in Israel, both of whom are subject to great migration-related social change, were said to show a rapidly increasing incidence of heart infarction.

Lystad (1957) and Jaco (1959) found an association between downward social mobility and mental illness but not between the latter and geographic mobility for the same populations. Other studies

(Hollingshead and Redlich, 1954, 1955, 1958; Lapouse et al., 1956; and Clausen and Kohn, 1959) demonstrated associations between mental illness and upward and horizontal mobility, accompanied in some cases by residential mobility, in some cases not.

Certain *chronic diseases* have been associated with migration status. As summarized by Myers (1969), the evidence on coronary heart disease indicates higher rates for rural to urban migrants than for native urbanites in certain United States cities (Syme et al., 1965). In a series of publications based on a national study in the United States, Haenzel et al. (1960, 1964) found that mortality from lung cancer is higher among urban residents born in rural areas than in lifetime urban residents (with age and level of cigarette smoking controlled).

There have been a large number of studies on migrant populations with reference to the incidence and prevalence of coronary heart disease, chronic bronchitis, certain types of cancer, and cerebrovascular disease in comparison to population groups in both the country of origin and the country of destination (for a general review, see Kagan, 1969). While important in themselves, these studies seldom fully incorporate the various types of environmental and adaptive factors, especially those related to urbanization, that may be essential for explaining any differentials found.

The migration *process* seems to be more important than the *environment* to which the person moves. In an industrial city in North Carolina, factory workers who came from rural areas had a higher prevalence of various disease symptoms and a higher level of absenteeism from work than the second generation of factory workers (Cassel and Tyroler, 1961). Newly immigrated Zulus to Natal were found to have a higher prevalence of hypertension than the Zulu population in rural areas (Scotch, 1960).

In a Swedish study (Korpi, 1972) comparing the number of days on *sick leave,* male migrants from rural areas were found to exhibit higher absenteeism than persons born in towns or cities. The more urbanized the area to which they migrated, the higher the absenteeism. Females exhibited a similar trend.

Of course, disease is an end-point produced in only a minority of migrants. The quality of life can be influenced in other terms, too. Weaver (1963) reviews the handicaps of newcomers to urban life, emphasizing the following in particular:

☐ misinformation about job opportunities and cost of living;

☐ abrupt severance of ties with the home community;

☐ ignorance of institutions in the (new) urban community;

☐ impediments to communication with city people;

☐ educational deficiencies which, in urban occupations and life, represent insurmountable handicaps.

5.5 The urban-rural continuum

Differences in mortality and morbidity have been reported between rural and urban areas. However, the data are difficult to interpret, partly because interregional comparisons imply comparisons of conglomerates comprising both types of environments, albeit in different proportions. Also, almost by definition, percentage differences will be substantial only in age groups with a relatively low absolute mortality or with regard to relatively rare causes of death. In the age groups in which people "normally" die, or with respect to rather common causes of death, urban-rural differences can never be great. These circumstances should be kept in mind when considering such differences in morbidity and mortality.

As shown in table 6, (Carlsson, 1974) the *male mortality index* for Stockholm, the capital of Sweden, is higher than for any other region and is considerably above the national mean. Thus approximately 20 per cent overmortality for males in Stockholm has no counterpart either in female trends or in Göteborg or Malmö, which are the second and third largest Swedish cities.

Comparing the mortality index for various age groups in Stockholm and

Table 6. Mortality index for various Swedish regions. All causes of death.

	Males	Females
Stockholm	118	99
Göteborg	101	92
Malmö	105	89
Stockholm region	111	105
Uppsala region	100	105
Linköping region	97	104
Lund-Malmö region	94	92
Göteborg region	96	97
Örebro region	102	105
Umeå region	103	106
Whole country	100	100

Source: Swedish National Statistics 1964–1967; Carlsson (1974).

Table 7. Mortality index in various age groups, in Stockholm and in two predominantly rural areas

	Stockholm		County of Kristianstad		County of Jämtland	
Age group	Males	Females	Males	Females	Males	Females
− 1	99	104	104	103	93	104
1− 9	92	97	84	73	93	108
10−19	87	107	87	65	102	110
20−29	104	140	87	106	98	119
30−39	131	130	89	77	132	105
40−49	131	119	102	81	104	90
50−59	132	112	89	90	95	100
60−69	132	102	90	84	92	100
70−79	119	97	87	86	91	111

Source: Carlsson (1974)

Malignant neoplasm of trachea, bronchus and lung

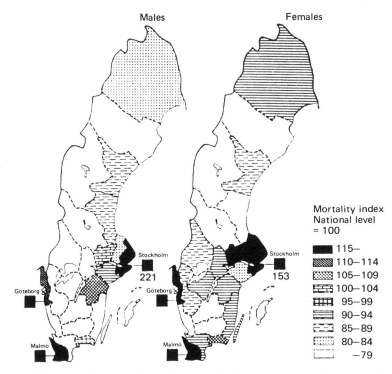

Figure 15. Maps of Sweden illustrating mortality index for malignant neoplasm of trachea, bronchus and lung by sex and county, 1964–67. (Source: Official Statistics of Sweden: Mortality and causes of death by regions 1964–67. The National Central Bureau of Statistics, Stockholm, 1971.)

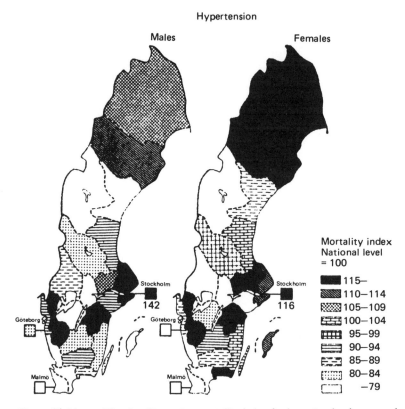

Figure 16. Maps of Sweden illustrating mortality index for hypertension by sex and county, 1964–67. (Source: Official Statistics of Sweden: Mortality and causes of death by regions 1964–67. The National Central Bureau of Statistics, Stockholm, 1971.)

in two predominantly rural areas (table 7), the excess male mortality turns out to be particularly marked between the ages of 30 and 69.

Analyzing the various *causes of death,* malignant neoplasm of trachea, bronchus and lung is considerably more common in the three largest cities (cf. figure 15). Mortality in peptic ulcer is about 50 per cent above the normal for males and is also elevated for the female population. Similarly, death from hypertension (cf. figure 16) and suicide (cf. figure 17) in Stockholm are considerably above the national means. As emphasized above, however, the most common causes of death exhibit no more than minor urban-rural differences; nor indeed, can they do so, because all people have to die from one cause or another. In particular, this applies to arteriosclerotic and degenerative heart diseases, the main

Suicide and self-inflicted injury

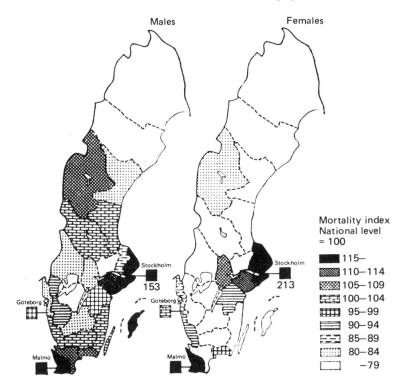

Figure 17. Maps of Sweden illustrating mortality index for suicide and selfinflicted injury by sex and county, 1964–67. (Source: Official Statistics of Sweden: Mortality and causes of death by regions 1964-67. The National Central Bureau of Statistics, Stockholm, 1971.)

cause of death in most developed countries irrespective of urban or rural habitat.

A comparison of the number of *days of illness* reported to the regional public health insurance offices for Stockholm and for the whole of Sweden, shows that the Stockholm figures are some 30 per cent higher. This difference may be due to many factors, including the greater exposure to communicable diseases, but also to psychosocial factors previously discussed. It can further be due to the better chances of obtaining medical care and staying away from work.

Studies on *blood pressure* carried out in every continent in the world (for review see Brod, 1971; Cassel, 1972) show that populations living in small, cohesive societies tend to have low blood pressures which do not differ between the young and the aged. In a number of these studies, groups who have left such societies and been in contact with western urban culture were found to have higher levels of blood pressure and to exhibit the familiar positive relationship between age and blood pressure found in studies of western populations.

In their recent very comprehensive review of *psychiatric disorders* in urban settings, Dohrenwend and Dohrenwend (1974) emphasize the difficulties of mapping psychiatric morbidity (first admissions to mental hospitals) in urban as compared with rural areas, for one thing because mental hospital beds are considerably less available to rural people, and because rural attitudes are such that even with mental institutions available, the rural family is more typically opposed to "committing" one of its members.

Taking these and other difficulties into account, the authors survey a very impressive body of information. From seven epidemiological studies comprising data from both rural and urban segments of the populations studied, they conclude that the *total* rate of psychiatric disorder is higher in urban settings, but that the differences are generally small. However, this partly reflects the circumstance that psychoses tend to be more common in rural areas, whereas neuroses and personality disorders are more usual in urban settings.

The authors draw attention to this differential morbidity, emphasizing that the interaction of pathogenic genetic and psychosocial influences may be different in these three groups of psychiatric disorders. Discussing the possibility that the difference in morbidity as to neuroses and personality disorders might be explained on the basis of a selective migration, the authors conclude that there is no substantial evidence favouring this hypothesis.

They further conclude that it is at present impossible to tell whether it is the "terrifically harsh, intensely individualistic, highly competetive, extremely crude, and often violently brutal" social city life that predisposes to disorder in general, or whether the concentration of psychiatric cases in the slums in due to downward social drift of previously ill persons or of persons predisposed to become psychiatrically ill. Again the authors emphasize that the "different types of psychiatric disorder show markedly different relationships to social class and to urban vs. rural settings. These differences suggest, in turn, that social causation and social selection processes in urban areas must be very different for the different types of disorder." Briefly, then, the authors present data supporting the assumption (a) that the *total* incidence of psychiatric disorders is somewhat higher in the urban setting than in the rural, (b) that the incidence of *neuroses* and *personality disorders* in the urban setting is considerably higher, and (c) that it is not yet possible to make any definite statements concerning the relative significance for this phenomenon of social causation and social selection, i.e. whether the symptomatology is generated primarily by the situation or by personality defect.

Comparing the self-rated *mental load* of blue-collar workers in Swedish rural and urban areas, Bolinder and Ohlström (1971) report a trend towards lower scores in sparsely populated areas and in communities with less than 5,000 inhabitants compared with larger towns and cities. It is not known whether this is due to specific conditions of work or to other characteristics of urban and rural life or to psychological differences between the two populations.

Johansson (1970) reports *subjective health indices* of a statistical sample comprising 6,000 Swedes of both sexes and presents the results in relation to the urban-rural continuum. In the Stockholm area, *fatigue* was reported somewhat more often than in any other area of the country. However, the differences were not pronounced and no clear urban-rural differences were found for any of the other physical and mental complaints.

The association between increased urbanization and higher *crime rates* is well known, but the causal relationships are difficult to disentangle. Crime statistics are very unreliable and hard to interpret. Nevertheless, in both the United States and the United Kingdom, for example, there is some evidence of a positive association between crime rates (serious crimes per 100,000 population) and city size. In the United Kingdom, crime rates are fairly similar in cities >200,000, though much lower in smaller towns (for review see Richardson, 1973). As emphasized by this author, the links between crime and population density are very complex. A few crimes (rape, assault, burglary) are lower in dense areas. Also, some sprawling cities (e.g. Los Angeles) have very high crime rates.

It seems that the criminality is related, not to the population density, but to associated factors. The welldeveloped transportation system covering the whole of a big city, including its surroundings, may contribute. In addition, potentially asocial subjects are probably attracted to big cities, with their relatively low degree of social control. It is also conceivable that urban life as such triggers off criminal behavior in people who, in a smaller population center, would have been able to remain better adapted. It has further been found that the maladapted in the urban conglomerate generally belong to the second generation of settlers, i.e. a group that lives in the city by inheritance rather than by choice. This likewise supports the assumption that the physical environment per se is less important than the social setting, or that urbanization may have late effects which should be mapped in studies covering several generations. This means that we must still wait for — and secure — feed-back concerning the results of the recent or ongoing wave of urbanization.

5.6 Some comments on urbanization and urban life

According to Dewey (1960), urbanization and *urban life* are characterized by five "inevitable accompaniments":

☐ *Anonymity:* urban people tend to be strangers to one another, contacts are transient and superficial. Not so with rural people.

☐ *Division of labour:* urban work is much more specialized than rural work and occupations are much more numerous.

☐ *Heterogeneity of life:* urban populations include a wide mixture of types, rural populations are more homogeneous.

☐ *Impersonal relationships:* these are normal in cities, but in rural places closer acquaintance is expected.

☐ *Symbols of status:* urban status derives largely from outward visible evidence: manners, speech, drugs, badges, place of residence, which is much less true of rural places.

Others have described urban life in terms of role conflict or ambiguity, status inconsistency or incongruity, cultural discontinuity, marginality and alienation, particularly as consequences of the migration process (McKinley & McKinley, 1972).

It has often been claimed that urban life constitutes a stressor with potential ill effects on health and wellbeing. Some evidence in favour of this hypothesis has been presented and will be discussed in the next section. Other evidence is to be found in epidemiological studies of *urbanization,* cf. e.g. Krapf (1964). In one of these studies, Tyroler and Cassel (1964) compared *coronary heart disease* mortality in two groups. The first comprised middle-aged male Americans of British ancestry, who had been brought up in rural surroundings but who, through rapid growth of the village, were subsequently exposed to urbanization and urban conditions, but without changing residence. This group was compared with a similar group of people who had been brought up exclusively under urban conditions. The *urbanized* group experienced a greater increase in coronary heart disease mortality in 10 years than the urban group. The possibilities afforded in this field by epidemiological research are discussed in more detail by Kagan (1971).

Tyroler and Cassel (1964) point out that health effects can be due to a great variety of influences, like changes in diet, level of physical activity, cigarette smoking, and meeting of deadlines.

The occupational environment can — but need not — be characterized by the geographical position of the place of work. Thus, high exposure to physical and/or psychosocial stressors can be found not only in cities and towns, but in typically rural areas as well. Such influences may further blur the effects of the urban and rural characteristics of the respective environment.

Noise is an important characteristic of life in crowded urban conglomerates. Again, human reactions to this exposure vary over a wide range. In an excellent review, Borsky (1971) mentions some of the main factors affecting annoyance reactions to noise: (a) when sounds interfere with desired human activities like sleep, rest, relaxation, conversation, listening to radio, TV or telephone, (b) feelings about the necessity or preventability of the noise, (c) feelings of the importance of the noise source and the value of its primary functions, (d) the extent to which there are other things disliked in the residential environment: cumulative dissatisfaction, (e) belief in the effect of noise on general health, and (f) the extent to which fear is associated with noise. According to Borsky, one of the most significant findings in repeated social surveys is that about 25 per cent of the variability in reported annoyance can be explained by changes in the noise environment alone. Differences of over 70 per cent can be explained by variability in personal attitudes and experiences.

The annoyance reactions possibly provoked by noise are usually accompanied by physiological stress reactions. Vegetative reactions can also be provoked in the absence of annoyance through the direct ramifications of the auditory nerve to the brain stem. There is even some support for the hypothesis that prolonged noise exposure can increase psychiatric and psychosomatic morbidity (for review, see Kryter, 1970; Nitschkoff and Kriwizkaja, 1968; Welch and Welch, 1970; Karlsson and Levi, 1974).

Sakamoto (1959) found that more than 50 per cent — a rather high proportion — of the habitants living close to an airport complained of various types of somatic distress, possibly induced by the aircraft noise.

In epidemiological studies, several authors (Mjasnikow, 1970; Andriukin, 1961; Shatalov et al., 1962; Ratner et al., 1963) report an increased incidence of *hypertension* in workers exposed to high noise levels. According to Mjasnikow, this increase in morbidity manifests itself after 8 years of exposure, reaching a maximum after 13 years.

Similarly, other authors (Jerkova and Kremarova, 1965; Andrukovich,

1965; Strakhov, 1966; and Dumkina, 1970) found an increased incidence of "nervous complaints" in workers habitually exposed to higher noise levels. Living in an area close to a noisy airport was accompanied by an increased number of admissions to psychiatric hospitals (Abey-Wickrama et al., 1969 and 1970). However, the causal implications of this statistical relationship can be seriously questioned (Chowns, 1970).

Reviewing studies on noise and mental disease, Lader (1971) concludes that noise exposure does not *generally* increase psychiatric morbidity but might be of some pathogenic significance in neurotic and anxious subjects.

Without necessarily leading to physical or mental disease, urban living can theoretically decrease the quality of life through many intervening variables, like longer *travel time*. The congestive traffic in many urban areas adds a considerable number of hours to the effective length of the working day, increasing fatigue and irritation.

The general environmental conditions of the large city are frequently at variance with the *esthetic standards* of the general population or groups of it (cf. Carlestam and Levi, 1971). Such conditions include defacement of buildings by vandals, littering of roadways and walkways, discoloration of waterways used for recreation, etc. Prevalent high population density often increases local wear and tear and the exploitation or even the overexploitation of nature resources. Effects of this type on water and air have become increasingly recognized, locally as well as globally. True, man tries to modify or even eliminate these effects by inventing countermeasures. He asphalts the ground, collects his water and food from more remote areas, and transports his foul water and garbage to remote recipients. In this way, our close environment has been made better – at the expense of our remote environment. We have shifted the problems but have not usually solved them. People in the industrialized countries often have clean clothes and a high hygienic standard, but at the expense of soiled nature comprising polluted air and dirty watercources. Our remote area has, by definition, become the close surroundings of our neighbour.

This *pollution* may have direct stressor effects by influencing the human body physically. It may further be perceived and thus elicit stress reactions more indirectly, e.g. by inducing fear of cancers caused by chemical agents, and of teratogens widely dispersed in our surroundings (Beard and Grandstaff, 1971). However, there are also examples of urban populations who deliberately seem to deny the risks inherent in environmental pollution. For example, in a survey of one city which experts claim to be a subject of serious air pollution, only 2.5 per cent spontaneously expressed any concern for air pollution, and 85 per cent considered the city a healthy place to live in (Smith et al., 1964).

What has been said so far concerning urban life should not been taken to indicate that cities and towns offer no benefits. Indeed, they do, and numerous people move to them voluntarily. Large cities offer a wider choice of jobs, social service and psychological and cultural stimulation. Salaries are usually higher, at least in Swedish urban conglomerates. Current discussion is concerned with the question whether or not these benefits are outbalanced by the environmental problems created by urbanization and urban life. Perhaps this discussion has contributed to a change in attitudes, especially in the young generations.

In a Gallup poll (SIFO, June 1971, published in the Industria Journal), a statistical sample from the population of 1 1/2 million young Swedish people (between 12 and 24 years old) were asked about their attitudes to urban and rural life. 96 per cent of those living in rural areas and 91 per cent of those living in small towns indicated that they did *not* want to move to a large city. About 2 out of 3 of the adolescents who were already living in large cities indicated that they would like to move away to a small town or to rural areas. There were no obvious differences in attitudes between different age and sex groups. In all, a minority of 14 per cent chose to live in a large city, whereas 42 per cent preferred to live in a small town, 41 per cent in a rural area and 3 per cent did not answer the question.

It is true that figures like these are difficult to evaluate but perhaps they do indicate that the continued and accelerating urbanization predicted by most authorities is not necessarily a "natural force" but – to some degree – a psychosocially induced behavioural trend which might change.

What has been said above has obvious implications for the structure of big cities. The many obvious advantages they offer are due, in part, to the large-scale production which the city makes possible because of its infrastructure and capital accumulation. The disadvantages associated with large-scale prodution tend to be forgotten and are usually not included in the cost-benefit calculations that precede political decisions for the distribution of industry.

It must further be emphasized that the present authors, like most others, usually refer to a system of norms specific for their own society. What is called a slum or environmental pollution – or a benefit – in Stockholm would not necessarily be termed so in Calcutta or London, respectively. The subjective experience may, however, be just as negative – or positive – in both cases, in spite of the obvious differences in purely physical terms. In general, we feel·that the relative importance of the objective, physical environment tends to be overemphasized. No doubt it is important, but social and psychological factors may be equally important.

5.7 Population density, and crowding

5.7.1 Some general considerations

As summarized by the National Academy of Sciences (1971), the commonly held view that high population density and crowding per se have deleterious effects on health probably derives largely from four empirical observations:

□ In some laboratory studies, deleterious health consequences have been noted as the number of *animals* housed together is increased.

□ Traditionally the densely populated (i.e. urban) areas have *reported higher death and morbidity rates*.

□ Industrialization and urbanization have frequently been followed by dramatic increases in death rates attributable to *infectious diseases*.

□ Studies of *military training camps* have reported exceptionally high rates of virus diseases.

As will be seen from this review, the evidence is very contradictory. One explanation might be as follows.

As repeatedly empasized throughout this document, man reacts with stress, distress and possibly disease not only to excess but also to deprivation of various kinds. If this also applies to population density, the relationship between various density levels and individual and social costs in terms of quality of life might well be U-shaped, the optimal density requiring the lowest costs and resulting in the highest quality (cf. figure 3). Such a relationship would explain the lack of consistent findings between population density and mental and physical health, because the relation is usually assumed to be more or less linear. As already emphasized, man's reactions to various aspects of urban conglomerates such as high density are further complicated and modified by his capacity for "social invention". In a densely populated environment, for instance, man may find some compensation in high material standards. If this new physical environment conflicts with his instincts, man changes his social situation by introducing various types of coping behavior, symbols or taboos, making his function in a social group possible and effective.

Our first question now is whether or not high population density *per se* creates negative effects from the psychological, medical and social points of view. Much of the debate on this issue has been based on *ethological research*.

5.7.2 Ethological studies

Animal studies reviewed by the National Academy of Sciences (1971) have demonstrated that physiological changes occur while the *population density* is *increasing*. These changes include adrenal and other endocrine secretions and a higher level of activation of the central nervous system. When the population has reached its maximum size and has adapted to the crowded conditions, the level of physical pathology drops to that of animals living in a not too densely populated environment. Deleterious effects of high density or social pressure have often been observed under *natural conditions*. Japanese deer, left to breed on an island off the Maryland coast, grew to a herd of about 300; within a few months, 200 died. Autopsies showed that the cause of death was neither malnutrition nor epidemic disease. Many of the dead animals had enlarged adrenal glands and signs of chronic kidney illness, and subsequent experiments have indicated that both these conditions can arise from stress and social pressure (NIMH, 1969). As reviewed by Galle and Gove (personal communication; for other reviews of the literature see Hall, 1966; Snyder, 1968; Wynne-Edwards, 1962) a study by Susiyama (1967) of wild monkeys indicated that high density led to a general breakdown in the monkeys' social order and resulted in extreme aggressive behaviour, hypersexuality, and the killing of young. High density appears to cause death in hares (Christian, 1950) and shrews (Christian and Davis, 1964).

Morris (1952) has shown *experimentally* that high density causes homosexuality in fish. Probably the most frequently demonstrated effect of density is in the area of natality. Under conditions of high density, for example, the clutch size of the great-tit decreases (Perrins, 1965), as does the number of young carried by shrews (Christian and Davis, 1964). It appears likely that high density reduces the fertility of elephants (Laws and Parker, 1968). Female house mice abort if they smell a strange male mouse (Chipman et al., 1966), as do shrews (Clulow and Clarke, 1968). In sum, density appears to have serious inhibiting effects on many animals. It must be noted, however, that the effect of density is not uniform among different species.

As summarized by Calhoun (1962) the experimental induction in rats of a population density substantially higher than that observed in their natural surroundings leads to "pathological behaviors": (a) increased mortality, especially among the very young; (b) lowered fertility rates; (c) neglect of the young by their mothers; (d) overly aggressive and conflict-oriented behaviour; (e) almost total withdrawal from the community; (f) sexual abberations, and other "psychotic" behaviour, even when food and water were sufficient for all.

Discussing such and other research data on crowding and quality of life, Stokols (1972) mentions that the applicability of data from *animal research* to the analysis of human crowding is limited by problems of ecological validity (Brunswik 1956), which arise whenever one generalizes from communities of animals to societies of men. Such generalizations are difficult, because man is a cultural creature, characterized by his ability to modify the environment and to innovate. On the other hand, ethological data permit the formulation of hypotheses concerning unfavourable behavioural and health effects in man in response to high and/or rapidly increasing population density. Let us now examine some of the evidence relating to such hypotheses.

Ethologists often define *aggression* as a behaviour tending to spread out individuals by repelling them from each other. If, as is often the case in urban conglomerates, large populations live together in confined places, a conflict might arise between this biological need for space and the lack of it.

As emphasized by Davis and Leyhausen (cit. Ardrey, 1972), the roomier the environment, the more likely it is that order will be achieved through territorial spacing; the denser the population, the more likely it will be that societies must turn to rank order as an organizing principle. The authors see dominance over a territory as guaranteeing the rights and liberty of the individual, so that territorial behaviour in man reinforces democracy. But with increasing density the role of absolute hierarchy increases proportionately. The authors argue that to a degree, hierarchy is always necessary as the essential instrument of law. But in the end, "overcrowded conditions are a danger to true democracy which it is impossible to exaggerate."

In many species of birds and rodents, crowding of strangers, especially in the presence of valued resources, such as food, sex or nesting locations, has been shown to increase aggression (Marler and Hamilton, 1966). Similar results have been reported by Hamburg (1971) in primates like baboons and chimpanzees. Comparing aggressive behaviour in forest-dwelling and city-dwelling monkeys (Rhesus macaque) in India, Lindburg (1969) reports much more aggression in the latter group, which has to compete with humans for food and space.

5.7.3 Survey studies

Whatever may be the influence of crowding on *human behavior,* it seems clear that spatial limitation involves potential inconveniences; cf the restriction of movement or the preclusion of privacy and isolation, due to the available amount of space per person and the way space is arranged. These potential constraints, however, are not necessarily salient to the individuals occupying a limited area. While the amount of space in a given area may appear limited to an outside observer, it will not inevitably seem inadequate to the occupants, especially if their activities do not require a high degree of behavioural coordination, if their relationships with each other are cooperative and friendly, or if they have had much experience of living and working under conditions of limited space. Such circumstances, then, would operate to minimize the salience of spatial constraints (Stokols, 1972). The same author points out that the particular form of one's response to crowding will be a function of the relative intensity of spatial, social and personal factors, and the degree to which they can be modified. Where the limitation of space is extreme, and restraints against direct alteration of spatial variables are low, the prepotent mode of response to crowding will be behavioural. For instance, the individual can augment his supply of personal space by leaving the crowded situation. In situations where either normative or physical constraints inhibit the overt behavioral adjustment of spatial variables, perceptual and cognitive modes of reducing the salience of restricted space will be more likely to occur. In such cases, the person may modify his standards of spatial adequacy, enhance the attractiveness of his task, or attempt to achieve a greater degree of coordination with others in the group, as a means of alleviating the sensation of crowding.

Although it has not been scientifically demonstrated, it would seem reasonable to expect, as do Galle et al. (1972), that persons would react to the incessant demands, stimulation, and lack of privacy resulting from overcrowding with irritability, wearyness and withdrawal. This effect might be particularly stressful to those already sick (or old) and in particular need of rest and relaxation. — It may well be that such additional irritation may be the final straw that breaks the camel's back.

Schorr (1970) reviews a number of effects of high dwelling density, mentioning inter alia fatigue and sleep deficiency. Continuos overstimulation, irritation and interruption my lead to unproductive expenditure of energy, which, in turn, ends in overfatigue. A study of working-class negroes in Chicago in 1945 gives an example of such effects. It revealed that most of these subjects slept less than 5 hours a night, simply due to lack of space for beds. High dwelling density also enhances intrafamily friction. This, in turn, may make family members spend their time out of doors. It becomes difficult for children to do their homework, and they spend much of their time beyond the reach of parental control. It has further been said that life in very large urban conglomerates leads to individuals eventually ceasing to function as mutually supporting members of a group.

5.7.4 Experimental studies

A recent social psychological study by Zimbardo (1969) is interesting in this context. The researchers bought a car and left it on a street near New York University. They did the same near Stanford University, located in a very much smaller city than New York. In both instances, the car was in a middle-class neighbourhood near a large university. In both cases, the hood was opened and the license plates removed to indicate that the car was in some difficulty. In the large city, the car was very soon broken up, whereas bypassers in the small town attempted to protect the car instead of damaging it.

Hamburg (1971) reviews two additional studies on interhuman relations in large cities, both focused on reactions to strangers. Altman and colleagues (1970) at the City University of New York, have been comparing the behaviour of city- and town-dwellers in their readiness to offer aid to strangers, aid that might increase their personal vulnerability and require some trust of strangers. The general observation of the investigators was that the people in small towns were considerably more friendly and less suspicious than those in the big city. In the other study, McKenna and Morgenthau (1970) compared the willingness of big-city dwellers and small-town dwellers to do favours for a stranger. The favour required a small amount of time and slight inconvenience. The authors conclude that people in the big city, whether engaged in a specific job or not, are less helpful and informative than people in small towns. This emotional climate in big cities has been supposed to decrease emotional security and to increase alienation, distress, and, consequently, psychiatric and psychosomatic disease.

Hamburg further calls attention to the fact that whatever else densely populated cities may do, and they clearly do a great deal, they do *crowd strangers* — beyond anything known in the past — on several scales:

☐ The vast *numbers* of persons.

☐ The *mobility* which relentlessly brings strangers into each city.

☐ The *complexity* of living which almost daily brings each of us into contact with many strangers, most of whom we will never see again.

Moreover, the modern city crowds strangers on this unprecedented scale in the presence of many *valued resources,* often perceived as likely to be in rather short supply: *valued objects, places, activities,* and *persons* — everything from parking space to sexual partners. It seems reasonable to conclude that rapidly increasing population density does, indeed, influence human behaviour and under some circumstances leads to a decreasing quality of life. Our next question concerns whether it also leads to ill health.

5.7.5 Epidemiological studies

In *epidemiological studies* of mental disorder, attempts have been made to correlate the incidence of defined disorders with high density and unfavourable social conditions. In general, it has been found (Strotzka, 1964) that diseases with a high hereditary factor, such as cyclic psychoses, show a uniform distribution over all areas. In contrast, schizophrenia and the phenomena of social disorganization, such as alcoholism, distinctly accumulate in crowded slums.

The following explanations can be given for such accumulations:

☐ Disturbed persons remain in such areas, while healthier ones move out.

☐ Others moving into such areas (drift theory).

☐ Environmental conditions partly cause mental disturbances.

☐ The local accumulation is related to other variables which are not mentioned above, such as social mobility and status, level of aspiration, etc.

As pointed out by Strotzka, all four possibilities occur, as individual case studies show, and it doubtless depends on the local conditions whether one of them prevails or a mixture.

If mental or somatic disease is our criterion of the ill effects of *high population density,* it becomes essential to find out at what levels it becomes critical. However, as emphasized by Querido (1964), we have not the slightest idea how much physical space a human being requires in order to function satisfactorily and to supply his needs. It would probably be not much more than the dimensions of a small cell. Chombart de Lauwe (1968) has attempted to give such critical values for crowding and overcrowding, probably based primarily on clinical impressions. According to this author, 16 sq.m is an essential minimum of space for each person. Disorders begin to appear below 14 sq.m. Severe disorders and antisocial activity are found below 8–10 sq.m. However, these thresholds surely do not apply to all ages, individuals and conditions of life.

Clearly, there must be some critical upper limits to population density. However, in the great majority of cases, these limits are set not by physical but by psychosocial factors. This is reflected in data reviewed by Dohrenwend and Dohrenwend (1974), for example in a study of the relationship between population density on the one hand and psychosomatic and social pathology on the other in the city that has probably the highest residential densities ever known in the world, namely Hong Kong. Citing this study (Mitchell, 1971), they point out that "the median size dwelling unit in the urbanized areas of the colony has 400 square feet (= 37 sq.m), and the median square feet per person is 43 (= 4 sq.m). Thirtynine per cent of the Hong Kong respondents report that they share their dwelling unit with non-kinsmen; 28 per cent sleep three or more to a bed; 13 per cent sleep four or more to a bed. . . They are also most likely to have only one room per unit, to have ten or more people in the unit, and to have two or more unrelated families sharing the same unit." Not even under such conditions was a relationship found between density *per se* and measures of "strain" except for one effect of considerable potential importance, namely parental supervision of children.

Schmitt (1966) correlated five density measures to nine indicators of low *quality of life:* death rate, suicide rate, infant mortality, admissions to mental hospitals, illegitimate birth, venereal disease, tuberculosis rate, juvenile delinquency and adult crime rate. With the exception of household size, all density measures correlated positively to the indicators, population per acre most strongly. Winsborough (1965) likewise found a strong correlation between density per acre and the "indicators". Similarly, the Chicago study by Galle et al. (1972) analyses the realtionship between demographic data and five pathology variables. This study shows that social structural variables (social class and ethnicity in particular) account for a substantial proportion of the relationship between density and pathologies. The multiple correlations between density variables and the pathologies ranges between 0.92 and 0.69, but when social class and ethnicity were controlled, the range dropped to between 0.58 and 0.37. Galle et al. also analyzed overall density into a set of components and found that persons per room correlated most highly with the pathologies. Mental illness pathology was related to another component of density, rooms per housing unit.

According to the National Academy of Sciences (1971), there is evidence that high population density has other injurious effects, occurring primarily during a *rapid increase* in its degree and extent. The effects appear to be much less serious when the increase is slow and the population is given sufficient time to adapt.

When interpreting results such as these, it is important to remember that the effects of high or rapidly changing population density can be expressed in widely different "languages", with reference to diverse value systems. What may be a disadvantage for one individual might be highly desirable from the viewpoint of society. Psychological advantages (e.g. the presence of pleasant excitement, challenge etc.) may be accompanied by medical disadvantages, at least in the longer run, e.g. by an increased "rate of wear and tear in the organism" and thus increasing morbidity. On the other hand, environmental stimuli which are clearly beneficial from the medical viewpoint (e.g. a certain regimen) may be experienced as clearly unpleasant. An advantage in economic terms may be counterbalanced by a psychological and medical disadvantage, and vice versa. Accordingly, before stating that environmental stimuli − e.g. those created by high or rapidly changing population density − are accompanied by disadvantageous phenomena, one must state the value system or systems applied, because different value systems may, and very often do, conflict.

5.8 Reproductive behaviour; nutrition

So far our review has delt with population density and change as well as with migration as stressors potentially provoking a decrease in health and wellbeing. However, various aspects of the *reproductive process* leading to − and being a function of − high and/or increasing population density can also contribute more directly.

It is well known that, for example, many births at short intervals as well as maternal ages below 18 or above 35 years, are associated with health risks such as fetal loss, stillbirth, perinatal mortality, prematurity, infant and childhood mortality, malnutrition and infection, and retarded physical and intellectual growth of children. The chances of survival are better for earlier-born children than for later-born, with the exception of the first-born child. From the second child onwards, the risk of death increases with increasing birth order, particularly after the fourth child. These effects are due to biological as well as social factors. The latter should not be overemphasized, because this relationship is found in every social class (cf. Omran, 1974). Briefly, then, major risk factors in this area comprise the number of children, the interval between pregnancies and the mother's age at pregnancy. At birth intervals of less than one year, the risk of complications is relatively high, being less so for intervals between one and two years. A combination of short birth intervals and low maternal age aggravates risks to the child's health.

These risks are not confined to the offspring. It is well known (cf. Omran, 1974) that high parity increases the risk of the mother dying during pregnancy, labour and puerperium. These women are also at higher risk of developing diabetes, cancer of the cervix, rheumatoid arthritis, hypertension, malnutrition and chronic ill-health. The same author also mentions that *fathers* of large families are more likely to develop hypertension and gastric ulcer.

Many of these effects are further amplified by *malnutrition* of the mother, child or both. Again we find this interconnectedness between various sets of variables. Malnutrition is a major determinant of these high death rates (Scrimshaw, 1974). On the other hand, high infant mortality makes parents reluctant to limit the size of their families. Further, large families often increase the burden on all family members, accentuating the malnutrition. Finally, if either of the parents dies or becomes permanently disabled due to high parity, malnutrition or both, this often leads to a critical deterioration in the health of the dependants.

As rightly emphasized by Winston Churchill, "there is no finer investment for any community than putting milk into babies". It is, indeed, one of the major collective tasks of all mankind to make this milk available universally.

6 The interrelatedness of total man and total environment – concluding remarks

6.1 The holistic and ecological approaches

Promoting an increased quality of life requires coordinated action in all major scientific and political areas (cf. United Nations, 1974). On the international level, a number of strategies have been formulated within the framework of this general objective. They comprise a number of complementary world plans, such as

☐ the FAO Indicative World Plan, and the World Food Program;

☐ the ILO World Employment Program;

☐ the Declaration of the United Nations Conference on the Human Environment;

☐ the United Nations World Plan of Action for the Application of Science and Technology to Development, and

☐ the International Development Strategy for the Second United Nations Development Decade.

Together with the proposed *World Population Plan of Action* (United Nations, 1974), these plans form a system of international strategies, plans and programs, which, taken together, could and should constitute an *overall strategy* of the international community for the promotion of a good quality of life.

Each of these plans, important as it may be, must be viewed in a holistic and ecological perspective. What may be good from one point of view (say, economy) may be bad from another (say, health), and vice versa. Correspondingly, what may be good for one component in the ecosystem (e.g. economic growth due to rapid industrialization) can be bad for another (e.g. because of the resulting rapid urbanization and disruption of cultural patterns and family ties).

Accordingly, the only rational approach is to *integrate all specialized strategies,* taking into account the entire ecosystem, and continuously *evaluating the outcome* not just in economic terms, or technological, or in terms of physical, or mental, or social wellbeing, but concomitantly in *all* these measures. Briefly, this combined holistic and ecological approach integrates all aspects of human wellbeing (physical, mental, social) with the corresponding aspects of the human environment. This strategy applies to political decision making, social action and evaluative research alike. Optimally, also these three processes could and should be integrated. These notions have received strong and clear-cut support at the recent Technical Discussion of the 27th World Health Assembly (WHO, 1974 a).

6.2 The cellular, individual and community levels

Repeated reference has been made to the ecological approach to human wellbeing. By this we mean the science and study of the reciprocal relationships between organisms and their environments. These relationships can be described at various levels of complexity. The basic unit in the system can be e.g. a cell, an organ, an organism, or e.g. a primary group, a community or even a nation. The optimal function of the entire system depends on a balance between functions on all these levels. If, for example, a group of cells begins to grow uncontrollably, the organism may be destroyed. It may be tempting to compare this process with grossly exploitive, egoistic behaviour on a social level, be it by individuals or groups (cf. Lorenz, 1973). But such an analogy is not directly admissable, although individuals or groups may indeed be exploiting or terrorizing other human beings and this may result in societal disintegration and human suffering. This brings us back to our initial emphasis on the need to define what is good or bad by adding the questions: (a) for whom?, (b) in which way?, (c) when? and (d) under which circumstances? Failure to take this into account, be it at community, national, international or any other level, may result in severe confusion.

6.3 Different – and conflicting – criteria for quality of life

The concept of quality of life has been defined (cf. page 16) and discussed (cf. paragraph 5.2, page 64). It has been emphasized that this concept is closely related to the WHO definition of health and that it depends primarily on the fit, or match, between situational characteristics (demands and opportunities) and the individual's abilities, needs and expectations as perceived by the individual himself. It has further been pointed out that this concept is in no way identical – though clearly related – to the level of living. The two concepts need not and indeed must not be mutually exclusive. To improve human wellbeing, decision-makers need a continuous feedback from grass-root level concerning *both* types of information. To exclude level of living might lead to so-called *"manipulated wellbeing"*, i.e. the individual is made to believe that this is the best of universes, even though the objective truth indicates otherwise. On the other hand, it is non-sensical to deny the enormous importance of psychosocial factors, e.g. man's expectations. Confronted with an *"expectation explosion"*, decision-makers might find that whatever they do to improve various aspects of the level of living, expectations often rise more rapidly than resources, and the widening gap between ambition and reality results in increasing dissatisfaction, seemingly paradoxically in view of the simultaneous rise in level of living. Accordingly, quality of life is profoundly dependent not only on objective reality but also on the individual's perception of this reality and on his expectations and coping in relation to it. True, expectations can be "manipulated" and abused, and indeed they are. But, the fact that satisfaction can be manipulated and abused does not invalidate the concept and its inclusion in coordinated world strategies. We belive that each individual can be assumed to be the best judge of his own situation and state of wellbeing. The alternative is some type of "big brother" who makes the evaluation for groups or nations. World history provides many examples of such "expert" or "elitiste" opinions being at variance with what was experienced by the man in the street.

Different weights can be attached to man's need satisfaction. Maslow (1954) has subdivided human needs into a three-tiered hierarchy. Our most essential needs have to do with survival. Our social needs relate to security and community, while the ego-related needs concern self-realisation. There will obviously be a tendency to ignore other needs until those relating to survival have been more or less satisfied. Or, as expressed by Berthold Brecht, "erst kommt das Fressen, dann kommt die Moral".

Accordingly, in the past, governments all over the world were largely preoccupied with reducing *mortality* rates, and rightly so. Now, however, increasing attention is being paid also to improving the quality of life by reducing *morbidity* and enhancing physical, mental and social *wellbeing*.

Severely disabling, although not necessarily life-threatening mental and physical disorders are widespread in developing and developed countries alike. So are *distress* and *human suffering*. The latter, however, still tend to be accepted as characteristics of human existence to such a degree that possible countermeasures are liable to be disregarded. Although fundamental to most eastern philosophies and to the way of life of preliterate peoples, the "quality of life" concept has been dismissed by many in the industrialized world as vague and devoid of operational content. Yet recent experience of growing dissatisfaction with the conditions of contemporary life indicates that to ignore this aspect is to imperil each of our separate efforts towards meeting human needs (cf. Eisenberg and Levi, 1974).

Quality of life has many aspects. Having ensured the satisfaction of our most immediate needs, we expect a certain amount of security, freedom, equality, belongingness, companionship, information, participation, power and resources. In doing so, we tend to forget that a certain amount of one component often means relinquishing one or several of the others. The good life is a *dynamic balance* of satisfactions of all these components, a balance which cannot be determined by experts. It will differ from person to person and will *characterize each individual*. This must be kept in mind so as to design a policy with so much flexibility and freedom of choice, that each man is able to arrive at his personal combination. Clearly, we are still very far from this utopian goal.

6.4 Level of living and the revolution of rising expectations

At the *low* levels of living presently confronting hundreds of millions of people, each increase will pay off by raising the quality of life. Above this level, the cost-benefit ratio in terms of quality of life is much more difficult to predict. Again, the expectations of each individual and the type and magnitude of the *discrepancy* between these expectations and perceived reality will condition the outcome, in analogy with Charles Dickens' observation in "David Copperfield": "Annual income twenty pound, annual expenditure nineteen nineteen six, result happiness. Annual income twenty pounds, annual expenditure twenty pounds ought and six, result misery."

It follows that various reactions of dissatisfaction and annoyance or even disease may be provoked even in the presence of environmental conditions which the vast majority of the world population would consider most favourable and pleasant. Thus, at upper socioeconomic levels, even relatively "trivial" problems may induce such reactions. Among the under-privileged, similar reactions may – but need not necessarily – be evoked by environmental conditions such as inadequate lighting, improper maintenance of flooring, inadequate heating or the presence of garbage, rats and vermin, or from high or rapidly changing population density (cf. Radford, 1971).

Man's satisfaction with his environment is certainly related to his access to goods and services, but is also a function of his expectations, and the of discrepancy not only between his needs and environmental opportunities but also between his expectations and his perceived reality.

An interesting illustration of the importance of psychosocial factors is given in a recent study reported by Örtendahl (1974). Sweden was grouped into five categories along the urban-rural dimension. A statistical sample of the population from each category was asked to indicate their *degree of satisfaction and dissatisfaction* with access to physical, social and cultural public services. These services included

☐ Public purchase of land and physical planning
☐ Access to accomodation
☐ Availability of jobs
☐ Roads, streets and traffic
☐ Water supply and sewerage
☐ The school
☐ Day care nurseries and nursery schools
☐ Domestic help to families with children
☐ Homes for old people, pensioners' dwellings and rent subsidies
☐ Public relief
☐ Support for sports and spare time occupations
☐ Public libraries and other cultural activities.

In general, the objective truth is that in Sweden all these facilities increase in magnitude, quality and accessibility with increasing degree of urbanization. However, so obviously do expectations as to what should be available, Consequently, it was found that the combined dissatisfaction score (i.e. with all twelve types of public services) was much the highest in the most urbanized area (Stockholm) and decreased successively with decreasing level of urbanization, followed by a new increase, albeit a moderate one, for the most rural areas of all (figure 18). It follows that decision-makers should not expect satisfaction to increase

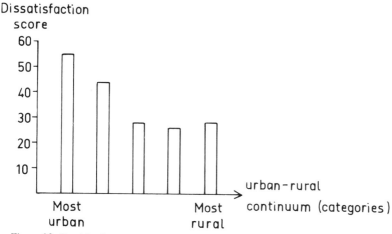

Figure 18. Combined measure of dissatisfaction with 12 services according to degree of urbanization. Sweden 1966. (*Source:* Örtendahl 1974.)

automatically when material standards and various facilities and services are improved. On the other hand, this is definitely not an argument against improving such facilities. It simply illustrates the enormous importance of psychosocial factors for the individual's experience of quality of life, partly because expectations are among those most easily influenced.

There are examples of countries in which the population has been brought to expect "blood, sweat and tears" and has gladly accepted this because it knew why such sacrifices were requested. In this way, a reasonably acceptable quality of life (from the viewpoint of the population) is maintained even in the presence of a relatively poor level of living (cf. also China's "great leap forward"). In contrast, populations can be manipulated and provoked to increase their expectations to levels clearly at variance with the limits set by available resources and by international obligations. Such a "revolution of rising expectations" might be a powerful instrument for social engineering and reconstruction. It can also be a severely disruptive and destructive force.

The outcome depends to a certain extent on the magnitude of the gap between expectations and perceived reality, and the rate at which this gap widens. Here, modern communication technology (including radio and television) plays a major role.

Part of the gap is further due to failure to perceive and/or appreciate reality. Reality often comprises qualities and benefits that are "hidden", or that rapidly tend to be taken for granted. Accordingly, not only the expectations but also the perception and appreciation of reality powerfully condition the quality of life. They can be — and often are — manipulated and modified, in a negative as well as a positive direction.

6.5 "Doomsday prophesies" — and passive homicide

Approximately one quarter of all the people who have ever lived are alive today. Whatever we do and however successful our programs for family planning, environmental protection, increased food production and a more equal distribution of resources, the world is no doubt confronted with a series of problems of unprecedented magnitude and complexity. World population today is approaching the 4 billion level. Not even the optimists believe that global zero population growth will be reached before the figure has risen to at least 12 billion. As repeatedly pointed out, population growth in developing *and* developed countries steps up the demands on limited resources. It also accentuates environmental problems dramatically. So does the revolution of rising expectations with regard to material standards in the *developed* countries. Developmental optimists who usually consider *just a single aspect* of this complex ecosystem, claim that new technologies will furnish solutions to all these problems, giving as an example that until quite recently fossil sources of energy were unknown to mankind. But they tend to forget that the question is not the acceptability of doomsday predictions. *Doomsday is already here* for all the hundreds of millions whose level of living is so extremely miserable that their quality of life is extremely low by all standards.

At the time of writing, hundreds of thousands of men, women and children in the Third World are starving to death, while the rich nations of the world stand by as relatively passive onlookers. The latter have the resources to save these people, but do not use them. This is nothing short of *passive homicide* on a gigantic scale, for which forthcoming generations will have every reason to blame those concerned.

And if this is *already* the case, how can we expect substantial changes for the better when the world faces problems of many times this magnitude?

What is needed is nothing short of *a revolution in international obligations and solidarity.* What is needed is a radical change in human attitudes, starting from grass-root level and progressing to those making the critical decisions on behalf of the governing bodies, including the super powers and international communities, before it is too late. Again, this illustrates the importance of psychosocial factors.

7 Monitoring and research for an integrated world plan of action

We use the term *monitoring* for several purposes. The first and most important, although most difficult to achieve, is as an *early warning system,* of impending trouble in the ecosystem in terms of level of living (cf. OECD, 1973) *and* quality of life at a time when something can still be done to prevent it. The monitor gives a warning, an "intelligence system" appraises it, a servomechanism translates this into a regulating need, the latter is applied through a regulating device. In our case the three latter steps must naturally be based not on automated "black boxes" but on *political decisions.* It follows that — having obtained this "digested" information and appraisal — the decision makers on all levels must be made receptive to the input offered. As things stand now, they do not always understand the signal, or they understand but do not care. If, however, the entire flow of events functions optimally, the threatened trouble is avoided through *social action,* and the monitoring system gives the "all clear" (Kagan and Levi, 1974).

But even when early warning can be given, there is often little avoiding action to take. For example, the present age distribution of the world population makes a further very considerable increase practically unavoidable. However, the warning may still be useful in that it gives *time for preparations* to deal with the problems envisaged.

Another equally important use of monitoring is to assess whether action to increase the quality of life is effective or otherwise, i.e. for *evaluation.*

In general, information for monitoring can be obtained from many sources — individual, family, special sub-groups (ad hoc sample studies, doctors' records, hospital records, factory records, parish records), community records, national surveys, statistics and plans, and serial photographs. It can comprise various population variables, various aspects of the environment — e.g. pollution and resource depletion, but also various components of the level of living (cf. OECD, 1973; see also pp. 61–65) — as well as the corresponding components of "quality of life", cf. WHO (1973); Kagan and Levi (1974). It follows that information must be collected from many disciplines, longitudinally and in a standardized way, to make data comparable over time.

The information obtained differs in kind. Thus, at one level, it may mean "this needs a closer look". At another it may indicate that environmental decay and/or a specific decrease in the quality of life is advancing at a specific rate towards or within the community. At yet another it may mean that ill effects have already occurred and action is needed to prevent their spread.

Since our knowledge of the effects of population density and change and environmental factors on quality of life is so incomplete, much of what we say about monitoring is speculative. Changes in population and environment which are likely to expose many people to new physical or social structures and processes, or generally necessitate many major adaptations, should alert administrators to the possibility of subsequent ill effects. This is so even when the changes are seen to be necessary from some points of view, or for some categories. There may still be "side effects". This possibility may be alerted at national, regional and local level, or from a smaller group such as a factory or enterprise. If this change in population or environment is likely to involve a removal from old forms of social support and either a lack of, or failure to use new forms, the likelihood that preventive action will be needed is further increased. Alertness to the possibility of quality of life hazards may arise from examining e.g. mortality and morbidity records and public opinion polls.

Such data are not likely to be conclusive in any way but high and/or rapidly increasing rates for suicide, neuroses and psychosomatic disorders, and/or distress, dissatisfaction and alienation would invite more detailed enquiry. Another somewhat speculative source of "warning" data might be juvenile delinquency rates and these may focus enquiry on a district, a class of people, a school or a family.

Clearly, many social, educational and health workers can be alerted to existing and impending quality of life problems. Preventive and therapeutic activities are initiated this way in many countries. We would like to see advantage taken of these activities, or interest in them, to initiate studies of their usefulness in accordance with our recommendations (cf. Kagan and Levi, 1974; Bronner and Levi, 1973). It is important to know whether any or all of these kinds of activity are effective in improving quality of life and to what extent they should be encouraged, modified or reduced. Greater understanding of the relationships between population variables, environmental variables, mechanisms, precursors, interacting variables and quality of life is likely to lead to ways of identifying high risk situations and high risk individuals with greater precision, and to ways of preventing ill effects in them, e.g. by offering them special support or by eliminating their exposure to or by modifying vicious conditions. This will probably call for special examination of many environments and groups of people. Some of the monitoring procedures referred to simply require an extended use of existing data. Others will require additional data obtained specially. This would be expensive but for the fact that much of the cost could be shared with social, medical, demographic and environmental services for other purposes. It is this overlap in expensive items – health and welfare workers, administration, premises, apparatus, secretarial staff, subjects, time – which makes importance of "comprehensive" health and welfare planning (cf. Rexed, 1971 a and b). Table 8 may furnish some basis for further discussion of psychosocial aspects of such planning (cf. also WHO, 1974 b).

Monitoring environmental stimuli, level of living and quality of life serves as an excellent basis for epidemiological research; and social action, if properly conducted and evaluated, can be regarded as part of a nation-wide or even international experiment. It follows that political decision making, social action and research should be closely integrated.

To maximize efficacy and safety and minimize cost, Kagan (personal communication) proposes a three-pronged epidemiological research strategy of conducting *prospective intervention community studies* to:

☐ evaluate health or social actions;

☐ at the same time *test key hypotheses* on the relationship between population variables, environmental factors and pathogenic mechanisms;

☐ at the same time, in the same communities of study, obtain quantified data on the *interrelation* of several other environmental, individual and group characteristics thought to be of importance for an understanding and control of the population-environment-quality of life system.

Table 8. Human needs and physical environment.

Needs		Dwellings	Dwelling Areas
Relatedness –'Love'	Responsibility & care of other persons	'Normal' amenities in the dwelling. No danger of physical harm to children. Suitable design for the old and physically handicapped	Traffic segregation. Free from pollutions Environ usable for physically and mentally 'handicapped'. Provision of 'normal' amenities.
	Respect for other persons	Possibility of individual privacy	Household's audiovisual privacy. Integration for different 'categories' of people.
	Knowledge of other persons	Possibilities of the whole household coming together	Clubs, sport centres, meeting places etc.

	Reproduction –sex	Aesthetically pleasant design. Audio-visual privacy.	
Transcendence –'Creation'	Children's education	Possibility of audio-visual privacy for the household. Space for education and playing.	Schools, churches, libraries, play areas etc.
	Material objects and Arts	Space for intellectual emotional and physical work for each individual.	Clubs, hobby work-shops, exhibition spaces, play areas etc.
	Ideas	Possibilities of audiovisual privacy for each individual. Space for reading & writing & discussing.	Libraries, schools. Discussion centres etc.
Rootedness	Brotherliness	Possibilities of coming together for the whole household. Entertaining guests	Integration of different 'categories' of people. Reduction of socio-economic inequalities.
Sence of Identity	Individual personality		Development of democratic institutions at all levels
Frame of orientation	Thought system		Theater, Dramatics, Concerts, Churches, Symbols, Libraries. Places of higher learning. Govt. buildings etc.
	Devotion objects		Churches. Religious buildings. Other symbols.

Source: Surya Kant Misra: Human Needs and Physical Environment – A Disscussion Paper, The Royal Swedish Institute of Technology, Stockholm (1970)

8 Summary and conclusions

8.1 Aims and scope of this document

The aim of this document is to depict how levels and changes in population density interact with environmental characteristics in their effects on the human organism in general and on various high risk groups. Population variables constitute our starting point. High risk groups are regarded as a target. Environmental characteristics serve as interacting variables, promoting or counteracting human wellbeing in complex interaction with population variables. Our end-point comprises various aspects of the quality of life.

Within this theoretical framework we have reviewed effects of high, low, increasing and decreasing population density and migration, interacting with urban and rural environments, industrialism, economy and employment, nutrition and cultural factors. High risk groups comprise infants and children, old people and the physically, mentally and socially handicapped. The effects are evaluated, wherever possible, in terms of quality of life, i.e. in physical, mental and social wellbeing as experienced by each individual (cf. WHO definition of health), in satisfaction and in man-environment fit.

The report summarizes interdisciplinary data concerning theories, research and other data on

☐ today's and tomorrow's population growth, population density and migration, particularly from rural to urban areas;

☐ other environmental factors potentially increasing the risk of ill health and reduced quality of life, particularly the urban environment, unemployment, poverty and malnutrition;

☐ population groups who are particularly vulnerable and at risk, primarily infants and children, old people and the physically, mentally and socially handicapped;

☐ the effect of the interaction of all these factors expressed in terms of level of living and quality of life.

8.2 Situation and trends with regard to population and environment

An account is given of the rather dramatic growth in world population, primarily due to the second stage of the demographic transition, i.e. high fertility combined with a marked decrease in mortality. Population growth is rapid enough to have been termed a "population explosion", based on the fact that world population has increased four-fould since 1800. Urban population, however, has increased more than 50 times, justifying the expression "the exploding cities". It is emphasized that space on earth is no problem in this context. The limits to growth are conditioned by

☐ lack of food,

☐ lack of energy,

☐ problems posed by environmental pollution,

☐ the enormous predicted increase in material standards in the developed countries, and the resultant "planet eating",

☐ the enormous and widening gap in resources between the developed and developing countries.

In addition, world population is facing migration on an unprecedented scale. Such migration often leads to drastic social changes and adaptional demands.

These processes often combine with exposure to poverty. Hundreds of millions exhibit a level of living definitely incompatible with a reasonable quality of life. Although the gross national product of developing countries is rising and the percentage may seem rather impressive, much of this is neutralized by simultaneous population growth. In addition, although the percentage increase per capita may still be impressive, the increase in absolute terms may still be rather low and the resulting level clearly unsatisfactory. The developed countries, on the other hand, seem to be governed by the belief that their GNP must increase ad infinitum with an accelerating rise in material standards. This results in heavy pressure on and a clearly inhuman use of limited resources.

Hundreds of millions of people are unemployed today. It can be safely predicted that this number will grow dramatically unless present trends are drastically changed. During the next three decades the developing countries will need at least one billion new jobs.

8.3 Doomsday prophesies and passive homicide

Between 300 and 500 million people are starving or malnourished. Although food production is increasing somewhat more rapidly than population growth, the balance is still very far from satisfactory, and the growth of food production per capita has decreased from the '50s to the

'60s. While this is being written, hundreds of thousands of people are starving to death. The developed countries have the economic means and the neccessary technologies to save them without having to make more than marginal sacrifices. In spite of this, they seem very reluctant to make use of their lifesaving potential, thereby actually committing what may be justly called *passive homicide*. This is nothing short of a terrible crime and must *never* be accepted or excused.

Developmental optimists are prone to ridicule what they call doomsday prophesies. They tend to forget or refuse to realize that *doomsday is already here* for a very considerable proportion of mankind. As emphasized by Adler—Karlsson (1974), in spite of all attempts to change the trends, the world has never seen so many adult illiterates as today, neither so many unemployed or underemployed or so many with no access to clean drinking water.

8.4 Population, environment and quality of life

Summarizing what has been said about the effect to various levels of population density in terms of quality of life, our conclusion must read that population density per se, unless extremely high or low, is not a major factor in influencing the quality of life. More important than areal density seems to be dwelling density, which can be very high not only in urban but also in rural areas. From the data found in the literature, it seems that the importance of density per se is exceeded by various *concomitants* of very high — or very low — population density, such as poverty and inadequate health and social services.

Nevertheless, high areal and dwelling density, particularly if combined with urban slums and squatters under conditions of social isolation and poverty, is highly associated with impaired quality of life. Uncertainty arises over which *component* or *combination* of components to blame, partly because they are connected. Nor should it be forgotten that the same physical conditions of high areal (or dwelling) density can be interpreted by some as proximity, fostering solidarity and companionship, but by others as crowding, constituting a threat to privacy and fostering competition and aggressive behaviour. Besides illustrating the profound importance of culturally determined attitudinal factors, this brings out the part played by expectations and perceptions of alternative ways of living. To quote William Blake (1757—1827), "man's desires are limited by his perceptions; none can desire what he has not perceived".

As pointed out, population change may comprise an increase or decrease as well as migration with no net change. Rapid population growth that is due to high fertility and low or decreasing mortality, results in an age structure which puts great burdens on the adult groups, particularly in the developing countries. Under conditions of scarce resources and malnourishment, combined with insufficient educational and work opportunities, a process is easily created which progressively accentuates the underprivileged status of successive generations.

A decrease in population, if critical, usually arises from emigration, which is generally selective; those most in need of support are then left in their original settings, while those most fit to struggle for life, to compete and survive, tend to be attracted to, in most cases, urban settings.

This migration from rural to urban areas has resulted in very rapid urban growth, often accompanied by still higher areal and dwelling densities in areas already densely populated, higher urban unemployment, the creation of urban slums and squatters and environmental deterioration and consequently a decline in the quality of life.

Particular problems confront uprooted immigrants from another culture. The completely new and different conditions that confront them produce a "cultural shock". At the same time, their impact on the host population is also considerable. This is particularly so when immigrants come from a wide range of other countries or are nomadic tribesmen, drugs users or foreign industrialists. To this cultural shock are added environmental stresses like pollution, inadequate housing and sanitation, insufficient transport facilities, inadequate recreational opportunities, inability of educational service to keep pace with the influx, limited access to resources and opportunities for certain high risk groups, unemployment, and the loss from rural areas of essential agricultural workers. Those who fail to assimilate are particularly prone to display various indices of a low quality of life, including mental and psychosomatic disorders, drug addiction, alcoholism, violence and crime. In spite of often extreme physical proximity, they tend to live as a "lonely crowd". The social isolation is often said to result in a sense of boredom, loss of identity and purposelessness characterizing alienation. For the urban poor this also often leads to the break-up of the extended family and the lack of a social role for the elderly. In addition, the work situation is frequently characterized by a lack of satisfying occupations.

8.5 Effects on social institutions

Accordingly, the effects of rapid population growth, of migration and urbanization, are also felt by various social institutions like the family, the school, the work place and the community. Family units become smaller, roles change and attitudes to marriage become less constant. The elderly often experience social rejection and loss of self-esteem. The young are often left without adequate parental control or care and with increasing confusion as regards norms and value systems, reinforcing the tension between them and their parents. Social groups lose or never establish adequate ties with their familial, occupational, religious and neighborhood communities. People tend to live uprooted, in anonymity, lonely and without purpose. The very young, the very old and the sick and handicapped tend to suffer in particular. The family's role in their care decreases, often without the community being able to take over.

The educational system frequently has difficulty in keeping up with increasing demands. Educational quality suffers, and the effects of this and of frequent changes of school and teachers all contribute to reduce the quality of life for schoolchildren.

At work, there is a similar lack of resources to absorb the enormous influx of unskilled rural workers. Even if wages are higher in the cities than in rural areas, work is often less satisfying and more monotonous. The employee often works shifts and under pressure, for long hours and exposed to occupational hazards. Transportation is often arduous, and personal relations with his fellows and management are frequently discouraged.

Effects of population variables are closely intertwined with those of other environmental influences. The latter differ greatly between countries or even within a country. This invalidates models that treat the world as a whole. Again we come back to our recommendation to formulate questions like: (a) good (or bad) for whom? (b) good (or bad) in which respects? (c) good (or bad) under which circumstances of a physical as well as a psychosocial nature?

In summary, we may conclude that population growth, alone or combined with industrialization, urbanization and urban life, has radically changed the living conditions of man. The decay or absence of improvement in terms of level of living and quality of life originating in high or increasing population density, in urbanization, pollution and "planet eating", are well documented. The action of such stimuli on mechanisms and precursors is still rather poorly understood.

8.6 Research, evaluation, monitoring

Before discussing prevention more directly, it would be desirable to know more. This means research. Nevertheless, there will no doubt be occasions when population, health, welfare, and community planners may feel, in the particular circumstances of their community, that action should be taken on the existing level of suspicion.

If this were to be the case, it would be important — in our opinion mandatory — to regard the action as a large-scale scientific experiment and to establish means of *evaluating* it for efficacy, safety and cost.

This has both a scientific and a social purpose. The former is to establish knowledge. The social purpose is to protect individuals from danger, and the community (and other communities) from unnecessary social and economic costs (cf. Kagan and Levi, 1974). It also serves to combat a false sense of security, to prevent delay in applying useful procedures and to provide rational support for innovative measures based on perceived cost and effect.

Such monitoring and evaluative research should be holistic and ecological in its approach, i.e. taking into account total man in his interaction with total environment. The results must be fed back to the politicians, whose obligation it is to decide priorities and form judgements without specialist bias.

8.7 Integrated world plans of action — a holistic and ecological approach

Within our very limited resources, time and printing space available, we have tried in this document to present a provisional basis for some of these judgements, trying to take population variables into account in the complex context of the entire ecosystem. We call attention to the very low level of living and quality of life already confronting hundreds of millions of people. Projections of future trends make us conclude that the various world plans of action (for food, water, environment, economic growth and distribution, education, family planning, health) must be integrated and put into force. They must be evaluated continuously, be interdisciplinary in their approach and focus on the only logical ultimate goal of the great majority of mankind, to help them attain at least a modicum of quality of life.

True, up to a certain degree man can tolerate crowding, poverty, hunger, pollution and loss of almost every one of his human rights and still survive. But he has to pay a price in terms of drastic decreases in "physical, mental and social wellbeing", i.e. in quality of life. In countless cases an incredible amount of human suffering is followed by the payment of the ultimate price, namely life itself. This may sound like just another doomsday prophecy. It is not. It is today's bitter reality for hundreds of millions of people. The truth is that we are presently committing homicide — albeit passively — by letting people starve to death. And we do so in cold blood. But the situation can still be changed. It must not be said of our generation by posterity that "we learn from history that we learn nothing from history". Hopefully we realize that it is now high time for the most decisive "revolution" — the revolution of international obligations, humaneness, and solidarity. We ought to be aware that this is the only alternative to the Götterdämmerung currently prepared for us by over-wise natural science and over-foolish statesmanship.

We can't possibly be expected to formulate anything like a general world plan of action for the improvement of the quality of life for all mankind. We feel, however, that most of the ingredients for such a plan are very probably to be found in the various specialized world plans already referred to in the text. We regard it as presumptious to propose exactly *how* these plans should be integrated with each other and the proper balance between them, for one thing because this balance will necessarily be different in different parts of the world. However, utilizing the benefits inherent in our interdisciplinary approach and our "birds-eye view", we would like to conclude by stating here some of our key points and recommendations.

8.8 Key points and recommendations

1. By all possible standards, the level of living of many hundreds of millions of people is so low (below subsistence) that their quality of life is bound to be intolerable.

2. To improve conditions by raising the level of living for these underpriviledged must be a top priority task for the international community.

3. Simultaneously, we need world-wide strategies to modify or change present accelerating trends toward population explosion, overurbanization, malnutrition, underemployment, poverty, environmental pollution, "planet eating,', illiteracy and inequality.

4. These tasks can never be achieved by one or another of the *specialized* strategies. These strategies should be *integrated* into a coordinated world plan of action.

5. For this purpose the psychosocial factor of *motivating* all people to a common global purpose is as important as a world plan and material resources.

6. Motivation is needed both for those who will give and those who will benefit.

7. A rise in level of living alone is not enough. Quality of life must also be taken into consideration. This means that an increased emphasis must be

put in social policy on psychosocial aspects, and on reformulation of societal goals.

8. Whatever may be the intentions, the outcome of separate or integrated world plans can never be predicted with certainty. To safeguard those concerned, we need continuous monitoring and evaluation to keep us on the course. This evaluation must be concerned with total man in his interaction with total environment. It requires close integration of national and international policy making and interdisciplinary research. Our future lies in learning from our failures and successes.

9. This should be the basis for the world population plan of action to be formulated in the near future.

9 Bibliography

Abey-Wickrama, I., Brook, M. F., Gattoni, F. E., and Herridge, C. F.: Mental — hospital admissions and aircraft noise. Lancet, 1275—1277 (1969).

Abey-Wickrama, I., Brook, M. F., Gattoni, F. E., and Herridge, C. F.: Mental — hospital admissions and aircraft noise. Lancet, 467 (1970).

Abu-Lughod, J.: Migrant adjustment to city life: the egyptian case. Amer. Journal of Sociology, 67:367—388 (1961).

Adler-Karlsson, G.: Some roads to humanicide (E/CONF. 60/SYM. III/23). Paper prepared for ECOSOC Symposium on Population, Resources and Environment, Stockholm Sept. 25—Oct. 5, 1973.

Adler-Karlsson, G.: Carrying Capacity and Harrying Capacity. A Contribution to the United Nations' Population Conference. Royal Ministry for Foreign Affairs, Stockholm, Sweden (1974).

Alberts, D. S.: A Plan for Measuring the Performance of Social Programs. Praeger Publishers, New York, Washington, London (1970).

Altman, D., Levine, M., Nadien, M. and Villena, S.: Unpublished research (Graduate Center, The City University of New York), summarized in *Milgram, S.:* The experience of living in cities. Science, 167:1461—1468 (1970).

Anderson, N.: The Industrial Urban Community. Appleton-Century-Crofts, New York (1971).

Andriukin, A. A.: Influence of sound stimulation on the development of hypertension. Clinical and experimental results. Cor. Vassa, 3:285—293 (1961).

Andrukovich, A. I.: Effect of industrial noise in winding and weaving factories on the arterial pressure in operators of the machines. Gig. Tr. Zabol., 9:39—42 (1965).

Antonovsky, A.: Social and cultural factors in coronary heart disease. Israel J. Med. Sci., 7:12:1578—1583 (1971).

Ardrey, R.: The Social Contract. Atheneum, New York (1970).

Argandoña, M. and Kiev, A.: Mental Health in the Developing World. The Free Press, New York (1972).

Baldwin, J. A. (ed.): Aspects of the Epidemiology of Mental Illness: Studies in Record Linkage. Little, Brown & Co., Boston (1971).

Barker, R. G.: Ecological Psychology. Concepts and Methods for Studying the Environment of Human Behavior. Stanford Univ. Press, Stanford, Calif. (1968).

Bates, B. C.: Territorial behavior in primates: A review of recent field studies. Primates, 11:271—284 (1970).

Beard, R. R. and Grandstaff, N.: The use of behavioral methods in the study of environmental agents. Working paper for the Forth Karolinska Institute Symposium on Environmental Health, Stockholm (1971).

Biderman, A. D., Louria, M. and Bacchus, J.: Incidents of Extreme Overcrowding. Bureau of Social Science Research, Washington, D. C. (1963).

Birren, J. E.: Physiology of Aging. Englewood Cliffs, N. J. (1964).

Birren, J. E.: Aging: psychological aspects. In *Stills, D. L.* (ed.) International Encyclopedia of the Social Sciences, Vol. 1. New York (1968).

Birren, J. E.: The abuse of the urban aged. Psychol. Today, 3:36–38, 76 (1970).

Blandy, R. and Wery, R.: Population and employment growth: Backue-1. International Labour Review, 107:5:441–449 (1973).

Blauner, R.: Alienation and Freedom: The Factory Worker and His Industry. The Univ. of Chicago Press, Chicago and London (1964).

Blenkner, M.: Environmental change and the aging individual. The Gerontologist, 7:1:101–105 (1967).

Bolinder, E. and Ohlström, B.: Stress på svenska arbetsplatser: En enkätundersökning bland LO-medlemmarna. Bokförlaget Prisma i samarbete med Landsorganisationen i Sverige, Lund (1971).

Booth, A. and Welch, S.: Crowding and urban crime rates. Unpublished manuscript (1973).

Booth, A. and Welch, S.: The effects of crowding: A cross national study. Prepublication draft.

Borsky, P. N.: Theoretical framework of factors influencing human annoyance and complaint reactions to environmental noise. Working paper for the Fourth Karolinska Institute Symposium on Environmental Health, Stockholm (1971).

Bose, A.: Rural development, dispersal of industries and population redistribution. Policies and experiences (E/CONF. 60/SYM. III/3). Paper prepared for ECOSOC Symposium on Population, Resources and Environment, Stockholm Sept. 25–Oct. 5, 1973.

Boserup, E.: The Conditions of Agricultural Growth. Aldine Publishing Co., Chicago (1965).

Bourne, P. G.: The Psychology and Physiology of Stress. Acad. Press., New York and London (1969).

Bradburn, N. M. and Caplovitz, D.: Reports on Happiness. Aldine Publishing Co., Chicago (1965).

Breese, G.: Urbanization in Newly Developing Countries. Prentice-Hall Inc., Englewood Cliffs, N. J. (1966).

Brod, J.: The influence of higher nervous processes induced by psychosocial environment on the development of essential hypertension. In *Levi, L. (ed.):* Society, Stress and Disease: The Psychosocial Environment and Psychosomatic Diseases, pp. 312–323. Oxford Univ. Press, London, New York, Toronto (1971).

Brody, E. B.: The Lost Ones. International Univ. Press Inc., New York (1973).

Bronner, K. and Levi, L.: Stress im Arbeitsleben, Musterschmidt Göttingen, Frankfurt und Zürich (1973).

Brown, L. R., et. al.: An overview of world trends. The Futurist, 6:6:222–232 (1972).

Brunswik, E.: Perception and the Representative Design of Psychological Experiments. University of California Press, Berkeley (1956).

Burton, T. L. and Cherry, G. E.: Social Research Technique for Planners. George Allen and Unwin Ltd., London (1970).

Calhoun, J. B.: Population density and social pathology. Sci. Amer., pp. 139–148 (1962).

Calhoun, J. B.: Psycho-ecological aspects of population. In environ/ mental: Essays on the Planet as a Home. Houghton Mifflin Co, (1971).

Calhoun, J. B.: Death squared: The explosive growth and demise of a mouse population. Proc. roy. Soc. Med., 66:80–86 (1973).

Calhoun, J. B.: Revolution, tribalism and the Cheshire cat: Three paths from now. Technological Forescasting and Social Change, 4:263–282 (1973).

Campbell, A. and Converse, P.: Monitoring the Quality of American Life. A Proposal to the Russel Sage Foundation. Survey Research Center, University of Michigan (1970).

Cannon, H. L. and Hopps, H. C. (eds.): Geochemical Environment in Relation to Health and Disease. The Geological Society of America Inc. Boulder, Colorado (1972).

Caplan, G.: Principles of Preventive Psychiatry. Basic Books Inc., New York, London (1964).

Carlestam, G.: Planning for a good environment. In *Levi, L. (ed.):* Society, Stress and Disease: The Psychosocial Environment and Psychosomatic Diseases, pp. 405–414. Oxford Univ. Press, London, New York, Toronto (1971).

Carlestam G.: Ekologiskt perspektiv på fysisk planering. Plan, 28:1:22–31 (1974).

Carlestam, G. and Levi, L.: Urban Conglomerates as Psychosocial Human Stressors – General Aspects, Swedish Trends, and Psychological and Medical Implications. A Contribution to the United Nations' Conference on the Human Environment. Royal Ministry for Foreign Affairs and Royal Ministry of Agriculture, Stockholm, Sweden (1971).

Carlestam, G., Karlsson, C.-G. and Levi, L.: Stress and disease in response to exposure to noise – A review. In Proceedings of the International Congress on Noise as a Public Health Problem, Dubrovnik, Yugoslavia, May 13–18, 1973, pp. 479–486. U. S. Government Printing Office, Washington (1974).

Carlsson, G.: Hälsa och lokal samhällsmiljö. In SOU 1974:2 Ortsbundna levnadsvillkor. Allmänna Förlaget, Stockholm (1974).

Carson, D. H.: Population concentration and human stress. In *Rourke, B. (ed.):* Explorations in the Psychology of Stress and Anxiety. Longmans, Ontario (1969).

Carter, N. G.: Population, environment and natural resources: A critical review of recent models (E/CONF. 60/SYM III/15). Paper prepared for ECOSOC Symposium on Population, Resources and Environment. Stockholm Sept. 25–Oct. 5, 1973.

Carthy, J. D. and Ebling, F. J. (eds.): The National History of Aggression. Acad. Press Inc. London, New York (1964).

Cassel, J.: Social science theory as a source of hypotheses in epidemiological research. Amer. J. publ. Health, 54:9:1482–1488 (1964).

Cassel, J.: Health consequences of population density and crowding. In

Rapid Population Growth: Consequences and Policy Implications, Vol. II pp. 462–478. National Academy of Sciences. John Hopkins Press, Baltimore (1971).

Cassel, J.: The Relation of the Urban Environment to Health: Towards a Conceptual Frame and a Research Strategy. Information Paper for WHO Expert Committee on Epidemiological Aspects of Housing and its Environment, Geneva (1972).

Cassel, J. and Tyroler, H. A.: Epidemiological studies of culture change. Archives of Environmental Health, 3:31–39 (1961).

Cassel, J., Patrick, R. and Jenkins, D.: Epidemiological analysis of the health implications of cultural change: A conceptual model. Annals of the New York Acad. of Sci., 84:17:938–949 (1960).

Cazzullo, C. L.: The dynamics of human ecosystems: An ecological study on suicide attempts among juvenile subjects. Paper pres. V. World Congress of Psychiatry, Mexico City, Mexico (1971).

Chalke, F. C. R. and Day, J. J. (eds.): Primary Prevention of Psychiatric Disorders. Univ. of Toronto Press, Canada (1968).

Cheraskin, E. and Ringsdorf, Jr., W. M. (eds.): Predictive Medicine. Pacific Press Publishing Association. Mountain View, Calif.; Omaha, Nebraska; Oshawa, Ont. (1973).

Chipman, R. K., Holt, J. A. and Fox, K. A.: Pregnancy failure in laboratory mice after multiple short term exposure to strange male. Nature, 210:653 (1966).

Choldin, M. H. and McGinty, M. J.: Bibliography: Population density, crowding, and social relations. Man-Environment Systems, 2:3:131–158 (1972).

Chowns, R. H.: Mental-hospital admissions and aircraft noise. Lancet, 467 (1970).

Christian, J. J.: The adreno-pituitary system and population cycles in mammals. Journal of Mammology, 31:247–259 (1950).

Christian, J. J.: Fighting, maturity, and population density in Microtus pennsylvanicus. Journal of Mammalogy, 52:3:556–567 (1971).

Christian, J. J. and Davis, D. E.: Endocrines, behavior and population. Science, 146:1550–1560 (1964).

Clark, C.: Population Growth and Land Use. Macmillan and Co. Ltd., London (1967).

Clausen, J. A. and Kohn, M. L.: Relation of schizophrenia to the social structure of a small city. In Epidemiology of Mental Disorder, pp. 69–94. Am. Ass. for the Advancement of Science, Washington, D. C. (1959).

Cleary, P.: Life events and disease – A review of methodology. Report No. 37 from the Laboratory for Clinical Stress Research, Stockholm (1974).

Clinton, R. L. and Godwin, R. K.: Research in the Politics of Population. Lexington Books, Lexington, Mass.; Toronto and London (1972).

Clinton, R. L., Flash, W. S. and Godwin, R. K.: Political Science in Population Studies. Lexington Books, Lexington, Mass.; Toronto and London (1972).

Clulow, F. U. and Clarke, J. R.: Pregnancy-block in Microtus agrestis and induced ovulator. Nature, 219:511 (1968).

Cole, H. S. D., Freeman, CH., Jahoda, M. and Pavitt, K. L. R. (eds.): Models of Doom: A Critique of the Limits to Growth. Universe Books, New York (1973).

Commoner, B.: The Closing Circle. Bantam Books, New York (1972).

Commonwealth Immigration Advisory Council: Report on the incidence of mental illness among migrants. Canberra (1961).

Cook, R. C.: World migration 1946–55. Population Bulletin, 13:77–95 (1957).

Day, A. T. and Day, L. H.: Cross-national comparison of population density. Science, 181:1016–1022 (1973).

Dalgard, O. S.: Migration and Functional Psychoses in Oslo. Universitetsforlaget, Oslo (1972).

David, H. P. ed.): Population and Mental Health. Hans Huber Publishers, Berne and Stuttgart (1964).

Davis, K.: The urbanization of the human population. Sci. Amer.,. 213:40–53 (1965).

Davis, K.: World Urbanization 1950–1970. Volume II: Analysis of Trends, Relationships, and Development. Population Monograph series, No. 9, University of California, Berkeley (1972).

Davis, P. R. (ed.): Performance under Sub-optimal Conditions. Taylor and Francis, London (1970).

Dewey, R.: The rural-urban continuum; real but relatively unimportant. Amer. Journal of Sociology, 66:1:60–66 (1960).

Djerassi, C.: Fertility control through abortion. Bulletin of the Atomic Scientists, pp. 9–14, 41–45 (Jan. 1972).

Dohrenwend, B. P. and Dohrenwend, B. S.: Psychiatric disorder in urban settings. In *Caplan, G. (ed.):* American Handbook of Psychiatry. Child and adolescense psychiatry – Socio-cultural and community psychiatry. II edition. Basic Books (1974).

Dosey, M. A. and Meisels, M.: Personal space and self protection. Journal of Personality and Social Psychology, 11:2:93–97 (1969).

Draper, P.: Crowding among hunter-gatherers: The ! Kung Bushmen. Science, 182:301–303 (1973).

Drewnowski, J.: Studies in the measurement of levels of living and welfare. UNRISD Report No. 70.3, Geneva (1970).

Driver, E. D.: World Population Policy: An Annotated Bibliography. Lexington Books, Lexington, Toronto, London (1972).

Dubos, R.: Man Adapting, Yale University Press. New Haven and London (1965).

Dubos, R.: Environmental determinants of human life. In *Glass, D. C.:* Environmental Influences. Rockefeller Univ. Press, New York (1968).

Dubos, R.: The social environment. In *Proshansky, H. M., Ittelson, W. H. and Rivlin, L. G. (eds.):* Environmental Psychology: Man and His Physical Setting pp. 202–208. Holt, Rinehart and Winston, Inc., New York (1970).

Dubos, R. J.: Humanizing the earth. Vital Speeches of the Day, 39:7: 206–209, (1973).

Duhl, L. J.: Urbanization and human needs. Amer. J. publ. Health, 54:5:721–728 (1964).

Dumkina, G. Z.: Some clinico-physiological investigations made in workers exposed to the effects of stable noise. In *Welch, B. L. and Welch, A.S.:* Physiological Effects of Noise, Plenum Press, New York and London (1970).

Dunbar, F.: Emotions and Bodily Changes. Columbia University Press, New York, (1954).

The *Ecologist:* A Blueprint for Survival. Penguin Specials, Suffolk (1972).

EFTA: National Settlement Strategies: A Framework for Regional Development. Secretariat of the European Free Trade Association, Geneva (1973).

Ehrlich, P. R.: Human population and the global environment (E/CONF. 60/SYM. III/6). Paper prepared for ECOSOC Symposium on Population, Resources and Environment, Stockholm Sept. 25–Oct. 5, 1973.

Ehrlich, P. R. and Ehrlich, A. H.: Population, Resources, Environment. Issues in Human Ecology. Freeman, San Francisco (1970).

Ehrlich, P. R. and Freedman, J. L.: Population, crowding and human behaviour. Scientist and Science Journal, April 1:10–14 (1971).

Eisenberg, L. and Levi, L.: Possibilities for WHO supported research in mental disorders at cellular, individual and social levels. Background paper för WHO/ACMR meeting, June 1974.

Eitinger, L. and Strøm, A.: Mortality and Morbidity after Excessive Stress. Universitetsforlaget, Oslo and Humanities Press, New York (1973).

Elliot, K. (ed.): The Family and Its Future. J. & A. Churchill, London (1970).

Engström, L.: Family planning in the socio-cultural context. World Health, pp. 22–27 (Jan. 1974).

Evans, G. W.: Personal space: Research review and bibliography. Man-Environment Systems, 3:4:203–215 (1973).

FAO: Third world food survey: FFHC Basic Study No. 11, Rome (1963).

FAO: The state of food and agriculture 1972, Rome (1972).

FAO: Population, food supply and agricultural development. (Doc. E/CONF. 60/BP/5). Background paper for the World Population Conference 1974. Presented at the United Nations Symposium on Population and Development, Cairo, June 4–14, 1973.

Felipe, N. J. and Sommer, R.: Invasions of personal space. Social Problems, 14:2:206–213 (1965).

Fenner, F.: Infectious disease and social change. The Medical Journal of Australia, pp. 1099–1102 (1971).

Frank, J. D.: Sanity and Survival: Psychological Aspects of War and Peace. Random House, New York (1967).

Frankenhaeuser, M.: Toleransgränser och livskvalitet. Plan, 28:1:16–21 (1974).

Freedman, J. L., Klevansky, S., and Ehrlich, P. R.: The effect of crowding on human task performance. Journal of Applied Social Psychology, 1:1:7–25 (1971).

Freeman, H. E., Levine, S. and Reeder, L. G. (eds.): Handbook of Medical Sociology. Prentice–Hall Inc., Englewood Cliffs, New Jersey (1972).

Frejka, T.: The Future of Population Growth. John Wiley & Sons, Inc., New York (1973).

Fried, M., and Gleicher, P.: Some sources of residential satisfaction in an urban slum. In *Proshansky, H. M., Ittelson, W. H., and Rivlin, L. G. (eds.):* Environmental Psychology: Man and His Physical Setting, pp. 333–346. Holt, Rinehart and Winston, Inc., New York (1970).

Frijling, B. W. (ed.): Social Change in Europe. E. J. Brill, Leiden (1973).

Fröberg, J. and Levi, L.: Stress and peptic ulcer in various occupational groups. In Proceedings of XVI International Congress on Occupational Health, pp. 71–73. Tokyo (1971).

Fröberg, J., Karlsson, C.-G., Levi, L. and Lidberg, L.: Psychological and biochemical stress reactions induced by psychosocial stimuli. In *Levi, L. (ed.):* Society, Stress and Disease – The Psychosocial Environment and Psychosomatic Diseases, pp. 280–295 and 454. Oxford Univ. Press, London, New York, Toronto (1971).

Galle, O. R., Gove, W. R. and McPherson, J. M.: Population density and pathology: What are the relations for man? Science, 176:23–30 (1972).

Gendell, M., Maraviglia, M. N. and Kreitner, P. C.: Fertility and economic activity of women in Guatemala City 1964. Demography, 7:3:273–286 (1970).

Genessee/Finger Lakes regional planning Board: The Migrant – A Human Perspective. Report No. 14, prepared for Department of Housing and Urban Development (1972).

Ginsburg, S. W.: A Psychiatrist's Views on Social Issues. Colombia Univ. Press, New York and London (1963).

Glass, D. C. (ed.): Environmental Influences. The Rockefeller Univ. Press and Russell Sage Foundation, New York (1968).

Glass, D. C. and Singer, J. E.: Urban Stress. Academic Press, Inc., New York (1972).

Goldscheider, C.: Differential residential mobility of the older population. Journal of Gerontology, 21:1–4:103–108 (1966).

Goldstein, S.: Socio-economic and migration differentials between the aged in the labor force and in the labor reserve. The Gerontologist, 7:1:31–40 (1967).

Goode, W. J.: The role of the family in industrialization. In Science, Technology and Development Vol. VII: Social Problems of Development and Urbanization. United States paper prepared for the United Nations' Conference on the Application of Science and Technology for the Benefit of the Less Developed Areas, Geneva (Febr. 1963).

Gould, D.: Paradox in Britain (Immigrants in Europe). World Health, p. 12 (Oct. 1973).

Greville, T. N. E. (ed.): Population Dynamics. Acad. Press, Inc., New York, London (1972).

Griffitt, W. and Veitch, R.: Hot and crowded: Influences of population density and temperature on interpersonal affective behavior. Journal

of Personality and Social Psychology, 17:1:92–98 (1971).
Grosser, G. H., Wechsler, H. and Greenblatt, M. (eds.): The Threat of Impeding Disaster. The MIT Press, Cambridge, Mass. (1964).

Haenszel, W., Loveland, D. B. and Sirken, M. G.: Lung cancer mortality as related to residence and smoking histories – I. White males, Journal of the National Cancer Institue, 28:947–1001 (1962).
Haenszel, W. and Taeuber, K. E.: Lung-cancer mortality as related to residence and smoking histories – II. White females. Journal of the National Cancer Institute, 32:803–838 (1964).
Hall, E. T.: The Hidden Dimension. Doubleday & Co., Inc., New York (1966).
Hamburg, D. A.: Crowding, stranger contact, and aggressive behaviour. In *Levi, L. (ed.):* Society, Stress and Disease: The Psychosocial Environment and Psychosomatic Diseases, pp. 209–218. Oxford Univ. Press, London, New York, Toronto (1971).
Hamburg, D. A.: An evolutionary perspective on human aggressiveness. In *Offer, D. and Freedman, D. X. (eds.):* The Field of Psychiatry: Essays in Honor of Roy R. Grinker, Sr. New York (1971).
Hance, W. A.: Population, Migration, and Urbanization in Africa. Columbia Univ. Press, New York (1970).
Hanna, W. J. and Hanna, J. L.: Urban Dynamics in Black Africa. Aldine Atherton, Inc., Chicago (1971).
Hare, E. H.: Psychiatric illness in urban communities. Paper presented at the Conference on the Influence of Urban and Working Environment on the Health and Behaviour of Modern Man, Prague (1969).
Hare, E. H. and Wing, J. K. (eds.): Psychiatric Epidemiology. Oxford Univ. Press, London, New York, Toronto (1970).
Harper, R. M. J.: Evolution and Illness. E. & S. Livingstone, Ltd., Edinburgh and London (1962).
Heer, D. M.: The impact of population density upon fertility: A comparison of human with animal populations. Paper prepared for Regional Seminar on Ecological Implications of Rural and Urban Population Growth, Bangkok (1971).
Hemmende strukturen in der heutigen industriegesellschaft. Dericht eines Interdiziplinären Symposiums. Gdi Verlag, Zürich (1969).
Heseltine, G. F. D. (ed.): Psychiatric Research in our Changing World. Excerpta Med. Foundation, Amsterdam (1969).
Hinkle, L. E. and Wolff, H. G.: The nature of man's adaptation to his total environment and the relation of this to illness. Archives of Internal Medicine, 99:2–20 (1957).
Hollingshead, A. B., and Redlich, F. C.: Schizophrenia and social structure. Amer. J. Psychiat., 110:695–701 (1954).
Hollingshead, A. B., and Redlich, F. C.: Social mobility and mental illness. Amer. J. Psychiat., 112:179–186 (1955).
Hollingshead, A. B. and Redlich, F. C.: Social Class and Mental Illness. Wiley & Sons, New York (1958).
Holst, D. von.: Sozialer Stress bei Säugetieren – ein biologisches Problem der Humanökologie. Paper prepared for the Werner-Reimers-Stiftung Conference on Human Ecology, Bad Homburg, April 28–30, 1973.

Hutt, C. and Vaizey, M. J.: Differential effects of group density on social behaviour. Nature, 209:1371–1372 (1966).

ILO: Asian employers' seminar on population and family planning (1971).
Ingvar, D. H.: Annoyance reactions – neurophysiological aspects. Working paper for the Fourth Karolinska Institute Symposium on Environmental Health, Stockholm (1971).
Ittelson, W. H.: Perception of the large-scale environment. Transactions of the New York Acad. of Sci., 32:7:807–815 (1971).

Jaco, E. G.: Social stress and mental illness in the community. In *Sussman, M. B. (ed.):* Community Structure and Analysis. pp. 388–409. Thomas Y. Crowell Co., New York (1959).
Jaco, E. G.: The Social Epidemiology of Mental Disorders. Russel Sage Foundation, New York (1960).
Jensen, M. M., and Rasmussen Jr., A. F.: Audiogenic stress and susceptibility to infection. In *Welch, B. L. and Welch, A. S.:* Physiological Effects of Nolse, pp. 7–20. Plenum Press, New York and London (1970).
Jerkova, H., and Kremarova, B.: Observation ·of the effect of noise on the general health of workers in large engineering factories; attempt at evaluation. Pracovni Lekarstvi, 17:147–148 (1965).
Johansson, S.: Den Vuxna Befolkningens Hälsotillstånd. Allmänna Förlaget, Stockholm, (1970).
Johansson, S.: The level of living survey: A presentation. Acta Sociologica, 16:3:211–219 (1973).
Johansson, S., Levi, L. and Lindstedt, S.: Stess and the thyroid gland: A review of clinical and experimental studies, and a report of own data on experimentally induced PBI reactions in man. Report No. 17 from the Laboratory for Clinical Stress Research, Stockholm (1970).
Juppenlatz, M.: Cities in Transformation. University of Queensland Press, St. Lucia, Queensland (1970).

Kagan, A. R.: Study opportunities – Studies of migrants in cardio-respiratory diseases. Paper presented at the Symposium on Methodological Aspects of Studies of Migrant Populations, held by the International Union Against Cancer, University of Hawaii, Febr. 5–13 1969.
Kagan, A. R.: Epidemiology and society, stress and disease. In *Levi, L. (ed.):* Society, Stress and Disease: The Psychosocial Environment and Psychosomatic Diseases, pp. 36–48. Oxford Univ. Press, London, New York, Toronto (1971).
Kagan, A. R. and Levi, L.: Health and environment – psychosocial stimuli. Report No. 27 from the Laboratory for Clinical Stress Research, Stockholm (1971 a). Also published in Social Science and Medicine (1974, in press).
Kagan, A. R., and Levi, L.: Adaptation of the psychosocial environment to man's abilities and needs; in *Levi, L.:* Society, Stress and Disease. The Psychosocial Environment and Psychosomatic Disease, pp. 399–404. Oxford Univ. Press, London, New York, Toronto (1971 b).
Kahn, A. J.: Theory and Practice of Social Planning. Russell Sage Foundation, New York (1969).

Kantor, M. B. (ed.): Mobility and Mental Health. Charles C. Thomas Publisher, Springfield, Ill. (1965).

Kantor, M. B.: Residential mobility and individual adjustment. Unpublished manuscript (Undated).

Kaplan, B. H. (ed.): Psychiatric Disorder and the Urban Environment. Behavioral Publications, New York (1970).

Karlsson, C.-G. and Levi, L.: Physiological effects of noise. Report No. 23 from the Laboratory for Clinical Stress Research. Stockholm (1971).

Kato, T. and Takahashi, T.: Family planning in industry: The Japanese experience. International Labour Review, 104:3:161–179 (1971).

Kempinski, R. and Krasnik, A.: Integration Problems in the Health System. Institute of Social Medicine, University of Copenhagen (1972).

Kent, D. P., Kastenbaum, R. and Sherwood, S. (eds.): Research Planning and Action for the Elderly. Behavioral Publications Inc., New York (1972).

Kiev, A.: Transcultural Psychiatry. The Free Press, New York (1972).

Kjellström, T.: Urbaniserings- och utflyttningspolitik. Dess påverkan på förekomst av psykosomatiska sjukdomar i befolkningen. Unpublished manuscript. (Undated).

Klein, D. C.: Community Dynamics and Mental Health. John Wiley & Sons Inc., New York (1968).

Kleiner, R. and Parker, S.: Migration and mental illness: A new look. Amer. Sociological Review, 24:5:687–690 (1959).

Kleiner, R. and Parker, S.: Goal striving and psychosomatic symptoms in a migrant and non-migrant population. In *Kantor, M. E. (ed.):* Mobility and Mental Health, pp. 78–85. Charles C. Thomas, Springfield, Ill. (1965).

Kleiner, R. and Parker, S.: Social-psychological aspects of migration and mental disorder in a negro population. Amer. Behavioral Scientist, 13:104–125 (1969).

Kolb, L. C., Bernard, V. W. and Dohrenwend, B. P. (eds.): Urban Challenges to Psychiatry. Little, Brown and Co., Boston (1969).

Kollath, W.: Zivilisationsbedingte Krankheiten und Todesursachen. Karl F. Haug Verlag, Ulm/Donau (1958).

Korpi, W.: Flyttning och hälsa. Mimeographed report. Department of sociology, University of Umeå, Umeå (1972).

Kral, V. A., Grad, B. and Berenson, J.: Stress reactions resulting from the relocation of an aged population. Canadian Psychiatric Association Journal, 13:1:201–209 (1968).

Krapf, E. E.: Social change in the genesis of mental disorder and health. In *David, H. P. (ed.):* Population and Mental Health. Hans Huber Publishers, Berne and Stuttgart (1964).

Kruse, L.: Ansätze zu einer Umweltpsychologie als Beiträge zu einer Humanökologie. Paper prepared for the Werner-Reimers-Stiftung Conference on Human Ecology, Bad Homburg, April 28–30, 1973.

Krystal, H. (ed.): Massive Psychic Trauma. International Univ. Press, Inc., New York (1968).

Kryter, K. D.: The Effects of Noise on Man. Acad. Press, New York and London (1970).
Kuhlen, R. G.: Aging and life-adjustment. In *Birren, J. E. (ed):* Handbook of Aging and the Individual. Chicago (1967).
Kälin, K.: Populationsdichte und Soziales Verhalten. Herbert Lang, Bern (1972).

Laborit, H.: L'homme et la Ville. Flammarion, Paris (1971).
Lader, M. H. (ed.): Studies of Anxiety. Brit. J. Psychiat., Special Publication No. 3. Headley Brothers, Ashford, Kent (1969).
Lader, M. H.: The responses of normal subjects and psychiatric patients to repetetive stimulation. In *Levi, L. (ed.):* Society, Stress and Disease — The Psychosocial Environment and Psychosomatic Diseases, pp. 417–432. Oxford Univ. Press, London, New York, Toronto (1971).
Lall, A. and Tirtha, R.: India's urbanization. Amer. Geographical Society, 19:1:1–7 (1968).
Lapin, B. A. and Cherkovich, G. A.: Environmental changes causing the development of neuroses and corticovisceral pathology in monkeys. In *Levi, L. (ed.):* Society, Stress and Diesease — The Psychosocial Environment and Psychosomatic Diseases, pp. 266–279. Oxford Univ. Press, London, New York, Toronto (1971).
Lapouse, R., Monk, M. A. and Terris, M.: The drift hypothesis and socio-economic differentials in schizophrenia. Amer. J. of Publ. Health, 46:978–986 (1956).
Lauwe, Chombart De. as quoted by *Koupernik, C.:* Psychiatry and the great city. Documenta Geigy, Man and Megalopolis. Basle, (1968).
Laws, R. M., and Parker, I. S. C.: Recent studies of elephant populations in East Africa. In Symposium of the Zoological Society, London (1968).
Lazarus, R. S.: Psychological Stress and the Coping Process. McGraw-Hill, New York (1967).
Lazarus, R. S.: Environmental planning in the context of stress and adaptation. In *Levi, L. (ed.):* Society, Stress and Disease: The Psychosocial Environment and Psychosomatic Diseases, pp. 436–444. Oxford Univ. Press, London, New York, Toronto (1971).
Lazarus, J., Locke, B. Z. and Thomas, D. S.: Migration differentials in mental disease. The Milbank Memorial Fund Quarterly, 41:1:25–42 (1963).
Lee, E. S.: Socio-economic and migration differentials in mental disease, New York State 1949–1951. The Milbank Memorial Fund Quarterly, 41:1:249–268 (1963).
Lee, D. K. K. and Minard, D. (eds.): Physiology, Environment, and Man. Acad. Press Inc., New York and London (1970).
Lehman, E. J.: Quality of life in the urban environment: A bibliography with abstracts. NTISearch report No. NTIS-WIN-73-003, (1973).
Lehnert, G. et al.: Spätfolgen nach extremen Lebensverhältnissen. Georg Thieme Verlag, Stuttgart (1970).
Leibman, M.: The effects of sex and race norms on personal space. Environment and Behavior, 2:2:208–246 (1970).

Leiderman, P. H. and Shapiro, D.: Psychobiological Approaches to Social Behavior. Stanford Univ. Press, Stanford, California (1969).

Leon, R. L., Martin, H. W. and Gladfelter, J. H.: An emotional and educational experience for urban migrants. Amer. J. Psychiat., 124:3: 381–384 (1967).

Levi, L.: Stress: Sources, Management and Prevention – Medical and Psychological Aspects of the Stress of Everyday Life. Liveright, New York (1967a).

Levi, L. (ed.): Emotional Stress: Physiological and Psychological Reactions – Medical, Industrial and Military Implications. Karger, Basel, New York (1967b). Russian translation, "Emotionalnij Stress", Leningrad (1970).

Levi, L.: Neuroendocrinology of anxiety. British J. Psychiatry. Special Supplement, pp. 40-52, (1968).

Levi, L. (ed.): Society, Stress and Disease: The Psychosocial Environment and Psychosomatic Diseases. Oxford Univ. Press, London, New York, Toronto (1971a).

Levi, L.: Vom Krankenbett zum Arbeitsplatz. Eine Einführung in die medizinische Rehabilitation und in die Arbeit und Berufsförderung Behinderter. Musterschmidt, Zürich, Göttingen, Frankfurt (1971b).

Levi, L. (ed.): Stress and Distress in Response to Psychosocial Stimuli. Pergamon Press, Oxford (1972 a). Also published as Supplement 528 to Acta Medica Scandinavica.

Levi, L.: Definition and evaluation of stress. Paper pres. II Congress International Society on Thrombosis and Haemostasis (Thrombosis et Diathesis Haemorrhagica (1972 b).

Levi, L.: Humanökologie – Psychosomatische Gesichtspunkte und Forschungsstrategien. Psychosomatische Medizin, 5:92–107 (1973).

Levi, L. (ed.): Society, Stress and Disease – Childhood and Adolescence. Oxford Univ. Press, London, New York, Toronto (1974).

Levi, L. and Kagan, A.: A synopsis of ecology and psychiatry: Some theoretical psychosomatic considerations, review of some studies and discussion of preventive aspects. Excerpta Medica International Congress Series No. 274 (1974).

Levy, L. and Rowitz, L.: The Ecology of Mental Disorder. Behavioral Publications, New York (1973).

Lindberg, G. (ed.): Urbana processer. Gleerup Bokförlag, Lund, Sweden (1971).

Lindburg, D.: Observations of Rhesus Macaque in Natural Habitats. Paper presented at Department of Psychiatry, Stanford University, Calif. (1969).

Little, K. B.: Cultural variation in social schemata. Journal of Personality and Social Psychology, 10:1:1–7 (1968).

Little, K. B.: Personal space. Journal of Experimental Social Psychology, 1:237–247 (1965).

Locke, B. Z., Kramer, M. and Pasamanick, B.: Immigration and insanity. Public Health Reports, 75:4:301–306 (1960).

Lohmann, H.: Psykisk Hälsa och Mänsklig Miljö. Socialstyrelsen redovisar, No. 30 (1972).

Loraine, J. A.: The Death of Tomorrow. Heinemann, London (1972).

Lorentz, K.: Die acht Todsünden der zivilisierten Menschkeit. R. Piper & Co. Verlag, München (1973).

Lystad, M. H.: Social mobility among selected groups of schizophrenic patients. Amer. Sociological Review, 22:3:288–292 (1957).

Malzberg, B.: Migration and mental disease among negroes in New York state. Amer. J. of Physical Anthropology, 21:1:107–113 (1936a).

Malzberg, B.: Rates of mental disease among certain population groups in New York State. Journal of the Amer. Statistical Assn., 31:545–548 (1936b).

Malzberg, B.: Social and Biological Aspects of Mental Disease. State Hospitals Press, Utica, New York (1940).

Malzberg, B.: Migration and mental disease among the white population of New York State. Human Biology, 34:89–98 (1962).

Malzberg, B. and Lee, E. S.: Migration and Mental Disease. Social Science Research Council, New York (1956).

Mamdani, M.: The Myth of Population Control. Monthly Review Press, New York (1972).

Mangin, W.: Mental health and migration to cities: A peruvian case. Annals New York Acad. of Sci., 84:17:911–917 (1960).

Marler, P. and Hamilton, W. J.: Mechanisms of Animal Behavior, New York (1966).

Marmor, J.: Mental health and overpopulation. In *Reid, S. T. and Lyon, D. L. (eds.):* Population Crisis: An Interdisciplinary Perspective, pp. 130–133. Scott, Foresman and Co., Glenview, Ill. (1972).

Marsden, H. M.: Crowding and animal behavior. In *Wohlwill, J. F. and Carson, D. H. (eds.):* Environment and the Social Sciences: Perspecitves and Applications, pp. 5–14. American Psychological Association, Washington D. C. (1972).

Maslow, A.: Motivation and Personality. Harper, New York (1954).

Mason, J. W. and Brady, J. V.: The sensitivity of psychoendocrine systems to social and physical environment. In *Leiderman, H. P. and Shapiro, D. (eds.):* Psychobiological Approaches to Social Behaviour. Stanford Univ. Press, Stanford, California (1964).

McGrath, J. E. (ed.): Social and Psychological Factors in Stress. Holt, Rinehart and Winston, Inc., New York (1970).

McKenna, W. and Morgenthau, S.: Unpublished research (Graduate Center, The City University of New York) summarized in *Milgram, S.:* The experience of living in cities. Science, 167:1461–1468 (1970).

McKinlay, J. B. and McKinlay, S. M.: Some comceptual and methodological issues in migration and the use of services. Paper prepared for the Third International Social Science and Medicine Conference (1972).

Meadows, D. H. et al.: The Limits to Growth. The New American Library Inc., New York (1972).

Michael, D. N.: The Unprepared Society: Planning for a Precarious Future. Basic Books, Inc., New York, London (1968).

Milgram, S.: The experience of living in cities. Science, 167:1461–1468 (1970).

Miller, L. (ed.): Mental Health in Rapid Social Change. Jerusalem Acad. Press, Jerusalem (1972).

Misra, S. K.: Human Needs and Physical Environment – A Discussion Paper. Dept. of Building Function Analysis, The Royal Institute of Technology, Stockholm (1970).

Misra, S. K.: User's needs, societal patterns and housing. Dept. of Building Functions Analysis, The Royal Institute of Technology, Stockholm, Report No. 3 (1972).

Mitchell, R. E.: Some social implications of high density housing. Amer. Sociological Review, 36:18–29 (1971).

Mjasnikow, A. L.: The pathogenesis of essential hypertension. Proceedings of the Prague Symposium pp. 153–162 (1960).

Mogey, J.: Sociology of Marriage and Family Behavior 1957–1968. C. I. D. S. S. and Mouton & Co., The Hague, Mouton, Paris (1971).

Moore, M. E.: Mortality and morbidity in the population. In *Riley, M. W. and Foner, A. (eds):* Aging and Society. Vol. 1, New York (1968).

Morris, D.: Homosexuality in the ten-spined stickleback. Behavior, 4:233–261 (1952).

Moser, C. A. and Scott, W.: British Towns. Oliver and Boyd, Edinburgh and London (1961).

Moss, G. E.: Illness, Immunity, and Social Interaction. John Wiley and Sons, New York (1973).

Mott, F. L.: Labor Force participation and fertility for women with young children in Rhode Island: An analysis of their interactions and antecedents. Reproduced by National Technical Information Service, U.S. Dept. of Commerce, Springfield (1972).

Munroe, R. L. and Munroe, R. H.: Population density and affective relationships in three East African societies. Journal of Social Psychology, 88:15–20 (1972).

Murphy, H. B. M.: Migration and the major mental disorders: A reappraisal. In *Kantor, M. B. (ed.):* Mobility and Mental Health. Charles C. Thomas Publisher, Springfield, Ill. (1965).

Myers, G. C.: Health effects of urbanization and migration. Paper prepared for the International Union for the Scientific Study of Population, General Conference, London (1969).

National Academy of Sciences: Rapid Population Growth: Consequences and Policy Implications. Prepared by a Study Committee of the Office of the Foreign Secretary (Revelle, R., Chairman). John Hopkins Press, Baltimore (1971).

National Institute of Mental Health: The mental health of urban America. Public Health Service Publication No. 1906 (Apr. 1969).

National Institute of Mental Health: Bibliography on the urban crisis by *Meyer, J. K.,* Public Health Service Publication No. 1948 (1969).

National Institute of Mental Health: Psychosocial consequences of population and environment. An experimental bibliography, Phase I. U. S. Department of Health, Education and Welfare (1974).

Nature (unsigned article): More coals of fire for Club of Rome. Nature, 239:5370:248–249 (1972).

Nitschkoff, S. and Kriwizkaja, G.: Lärmbelastung, akustischer Reiz und neurovegetative Störungen. Georg Thieme Verlag, Leipzig (1968).

OECD: List of Social Concerns; common to most OECD countries. Report No. 1 from the OECD social indicator development programme (1973).

Official Statistics of Sweden: Mortality and Causes of Death by Regions 1964–67. The National Central Bureau of Statistics, Stockholm (1971).

Omran, A. R.: Health benefits for mother and child. World Health, pp. 6–13 (Jan. 1974).

Parker, R. S. (ed.): The Emotional Stress of War, Violence, and Peace. Stanwix House, Inc., Pittsburgh (1972).

Parkers, M. C.: What becomes of redundant world models? A contribution to the study of adaptation to change. Paper presented at the Third International Conference on Social Science and Medicine, Elsinore, Denmark (1972).

Perrings, C. M.: Population fluxuations and clutch size in great tits. Journal of Animal Ecology, 34:601 (1965).

Pfeiffer, W. M.: Transkulturelle Psychiatrie. Georg Thieme Verlag. Stuttgart (1971).

Pipping, H. E.: Standard of living. The concept and its place in economics. Commentationes Humanarum Litterarum 18(4). Helsingfors (1953).

Plant, J. S.: Som psychiatric aspects of crowded living conditions. Amer. J. Psychiat, 9:5:849–860 (1930).

Proshansky, H. M., Ittelson, W. H. and Rivlin, L. G. (eds.): Environmental Psychology: Man and his Physical Setting. Holt, Rinehart and Winston, Inc., New York (1970).

Querido, A.: Population problems and mental health. In *David, H. P. (ed.):* Population and Mental Health. Hans Huber Publishers, Berne and Stuttgart (1964).

Radford, E. P.: Annoyance reactions to other environmental conditions or agents. Working paper for the Fourth Karolinska Institute Symposium on Environmental Health, Stockholm (1971).

Rahe, R. H.: Multi-cultural correlations of life change scaling: America, Japan, Denmark and Sweden. J. Psychosom. Res., 13:191–195. Pergamon Press (1969:a).

Rahe, R. H.: Life crisis and health change. In *May, PH. R. A. and Wittenborn, J. R. (eds.):* Psychiatric Drug Response: Advances in Prediction. Charles C. Thomas, Publ., Springfield, Illinois (1969:b).

Rahe, R. H.: Subjects' recent life changes and their near-future illness susceptibility. In *Reichsman, F. (ed.):* Advances in Psychosomatic Medicine, Vol. 8. S. Karger, Basel, New York (1972).

Rahe, R. H.: Life changes and near-future illness reports. In *Levi, L. (ed.):* Emotions – Their Parameters and Measurement. Raven Press, New York (1974 in press).

Rahe, R. H., and Lind, E.: Psychosocial factors and myocardial sudden death in Sweden. J. Psychosom. Res., 15:19 (1971).

Rahe, R. H., and Paasikivi, J.: Psychosocial factors and myocardial infarction, II: An inpatient study in Sweden. J. Psychosom. Res., 15:33 (1971).

Rahe, R. H., McKean, J. D. and Arthur, R. J.: A longitudinal study of lifechange and illness patterns. J. Psychosomatic Res., 10:355–366 (1967).

Rao, M. S. A.: Urbanization and Social Change. Orient Longmans Ltd., New Dehli (1970).

Rasmussen, J. E. (ed.): Man in Isolation and Confinement. Aldine Publishing Co., Chicago (1973).

Ratner, M. V., Medved, R. A., Filin, A. P., Skok, W. I., Rodenkow, W. F., und Makarenkow, N. A.: Thesen des Berichtes der Allunionswissen-schaftlichen Tagung über methodische Probleme der Lärmwirkung auf den Organismus. Institut f. Arbeitshygiene und Berufskrankheiten, AMW, UdSSR (1963).

Reid, D. D.: The future of migrant studies. Israel J. Med. Sci., 7:1592–1596 (1971).

Reid, D. D.: Studies of disease among migrants and native populations in Great Britain, Norway, and the United States. I. Background and design. National Cancer Institute Monograph, 19:287–299 (1966).

Reid, D. D. et al.: Studies of disease among migrants and native population in Great Britain, Norway, and the United States. III. Prevalence of cardiorespiratory symptoms among migrants and Native-Born in the United States. National Cancer Institute Monograph, 19:321–346 (1966).

Reid, S. T. and Lyon, D. L. (eds.): Population Crisis: An Interdisciplinary Perspective. Scott, Foresman and Co., Glenview, Ill. (1972).

Revelle, R.: Will the earth's land and water resources be sufficient for future populations? (E/CONF. 60/SYM. III/13), Addendum ditto. Paper prepared for ECOSOC Symposium on Population, Resources and Environment, Stockholm Sept. 25–Oct. 5, 1973.

Rexed, B.: Framtidens sociala miljö. Socialnytt No. 7, 2–12 (1971a).

Rexed, B.: Integrerat Samhälle. Socialstyrelsen redovisar, No. 21 (1971b).

Richardson, H. W.: The costs and benefits of alternative settlement patterns or are big cities bad? (E/CONF. 60/SYM. III/4). Paper pre-pared for ECOSOC Symposium on Population, Resources and En-vironment, Stockholm Sept. 25–Oct. 5, 1973.

Richmond, M. E.: Social Diagnosis. The Free Press, New York (1965).

Riley, M. W. and Foner, A. (eds.): Aging and Society Vol. 1. New York (1968).

Rioch, D. McK.: The development of gastrointestinal lesions in monkeys. In *Levi, L. (ed.):* Society, Stress and Disease – The Psychosocial Environment and Psychosomatic Diseases, pp. 261–265. Oxford Univ. Press, London, New York, Toronto (1971).

Roessler, R., and Greenfield, N. S. (eds.): Physiological Correlates of Psychological Disorder. The University of Wisconsin Press, Madison (1962).

Rogers, E. M.: Social Change in Rural Society. Appleton-Century-Crofts, Inc., New York (1960).

Rowitz, R. and Levy, L.: Ecological analysis of treated mental disorders in Chicago. Arch. Gen. Psychiat., 19:571−579 (1968).

Ruprecht, Th. K. and Wahren, C.: Population Programmes and Economic and Social Development. Development Centre of the OECD, Paris (1970).

Sage Urban Studies Abstracts: Vol. 1, No. 1. Sage Publications, Beverly Hills, London (1973).

Sakamoto, H.: Endocrine dysfunction in noisy environment, Report I. Mie Medical Journal, 9:1:39−58 (1959).

Sakamoto, H.: Endocrine dysfunction in noisy environment. Report II. Mie Medical Journal, 9:1:59−74 (1959).

Sangsingkeo, P.: Mental health in developing countries. In *David, H. P. (ed.):* Population and Mental Health. Hans Huber Publishers, Berne and Stuttgart (1964).

Schaefer, H. and Blohmke, M.: Sozialmedizin. Georg Thieme Verlag, Stuttgart (1972).

Schmandt, H. J. and Bloomberg, Jr, W. (eds.): The Quality of Urban Life. Vol. 3: Urban Affairs Annual Reviews. Sage Publication, Inc., Beverley Hills, Calif. (1969).

Schmitt, R. C.: Density, delinquency, and crime in Honolulu. Sociology and Social Research, 41:274−276 (1957).

Schmitt, R. C.: Implications of density in Hong Kong. Journal of the American Institute of Planners, 29:210−217 (1963).

Schmitt, R. C.: Density, health, and social disorganization. Journal of the American Institute of Planners, 32:38−40 (1966).

Schoor, A. L.: Slums and social security. Research report No. 1, Social Security Administration, U. S. Department of Health, Education, and Welfare.

Schoor, A. L.: Housing and its effects. In *Proshansky, H. M., Ittelson, W. H. and Rivlin, L. G. (eds.):* Environmental Psychology: Man and His Physical Setting, pp. 319−333. Holt, Rinehart and Winston, Inc., New York (1970).

Schulze, H.: Der progressivdomestizierte Mensch und seine Neurosen. J. F. Lehmanns Verlag, München (1964).

Scotch, N. A.: A preliminary report on the relation of sociocultural factors to hypertension among the Zulu. Annals of the New York Acad. of Sci., 84:17:1001−1009 (1960).

Scotch, N. A.: Sociocultural factors in the epidemiology of Zulu Hypertension. Amer. J. publ. Health, 53:1205−1213 (1963).

Scott, J. P. and Scott, S. F. (eds.): Social Control and Social Change. The University of Chicago Press, Chicago (1971).

Scrimshaw, N. S.: Food, health and family planning. World Health, pp. 14−21 (Jan. 1974).

Seligman, B. B.: Most Notorious Victory: Man in the Age of Automation. The Free Press, New York (1966).

Selye, H.: The evolution of the stress concept − stress and cardiovascular disease. In *Levi, L. (ed.):* Society, Stress and Disease − The Psychosocial Environment and Psychosomatic Diseases, pp. 299−311 and 453−476. Oxford Univ. Press, London, New York, Toronto (1971).

Shatalov, N. N., Saitanov, A. O., and Glotova, K. V.: On the state of the cardiovascular system under conditions of exposure to continuous noise. Report T-411-R, N65-15577 Defense Research Board, Toronto, Canada (1962).

Simeons, A. T. W.: Man's Presumptuous Brain. Longmans, London (1960).

Singer, S. F. (ed.): Is There an Optimum Level of Population? McGraw-Hill Book Co., New York (1971).   `

Slotkin, J. S.: From Field to Factory. The Free Press, Glencoe, Ill. (1960).

Smith, T. E. (ed.): The Politics of Family Planning in the Third World. George Allen & Unwin Ltd., London (1973).

Smith, W. S., Schueneman, J. J. and Zeidberg, L.: Public reaction to air pollution in Nashville, Tennessee. Journal of the Air Pollution Control Association, 14:418–423 (1964).

Snyder, R. L.: Reproduction and population pressures. In *Stellar, E. and Sprague, J. (eds.):* Progress in Physiological Psychology, pp. 119–160. Acad. Press, New York (1968).

Sommer, R.: Studies in personal space. Sociometry, 22:3:247–260 (1959).

SOU 1974:1: Orter i Regional Samverkan. Allmänna Förlaget, Stockholm (1974).

Spengler, J. J.: Technological transfer, population and environment (E/CONF. 60/SYM. III/5). Paper prepared for ECOSOC Symposium on Population, Resources, and Environment, Stockholm Sept. 25– Oct. 5, 1973.

Spooner, B. (ed): Population Growth: Anthropological Implications. The MIT Press, Cambridge, Mass. (1972).

Srole, L.: Urbanization and mental health: Some reformulations. Amer. Scientist, 60:5:576–583 (1972).

Stapleton, TH.: The change to a technological society. Pediatrics, 47:1:314–319 (1971).

Steigenga, W.: Urbanization and town planning. In *David, H. P. (ed.):* Population and Mental Health. Hans Huber Publishers, Berne and Stuttgart (1964).

Stokols, D.: On the distinction between density and crowding: Some implications for future research. Psychol. Rev., 79:3:275–277 (1972a).

Stokols, D.: A Social-psychological model of human crowding phenomena. Journal of the American Institute of Planners, 38:2:72–83 (1972b).

Strakhov, A. B.: Some questions of the mechanism of the action of noise on an organism. Report N 67-11646, Joint Publication Research Service, Washington, D. C. (1966).

Strotzka, H.: Town planning and mental health. In *David, H. P. (ed.):* Population and Mental Health. Hans Huber Publishers, Berne and Stuttgart (1964).

Susiyama, Y.: Social organization of Hanuman langurs. In *Altmann, S. A. (ed.):* Social Communications Among Primates. University of Chicago Press, Chicago (1967).

Swanson, H.: The consequences of overpopulation. New Scientist, 59: 856:190–192 (1973).
Sweet, J. A.: Family composition and the labor force activity of American wives. Demography, 7:2:195–266 (1970).
Syme, S. L., Borhani, N. O. and Buechley, R. W.: Cultural mobility and coronary heart disease in an urban area. Amer. Journal of Epidemiology, 82:3:334–346 (1965).

Tanner, J. M. (ed.): Stress and Psychiatric Disorder. Blackwell Scientific Publications, Oxford (1960).
Taylor, J.: The effects of population density upon correlates of emotionality and learning efficiency. The Journal of General Psychology, 80:205–218 (1969).
Theorell, T.: Psychosocial factors in relation to the onset of myocardial infarction and to some metabolic variables – A pilot study. From the Department of Medicine, Seraphimer Hospital, Karolinska Institute, Stockholm (1970).
Theorell, T. and Rahe, R. H.: Psykosociala faktorer i tidsmässig relation till hjärtinfarkt. Nordisk Medicin, 84:850–857 (1970).
Theorell, T., and Rahe, R. H.: Psychosocial factors and myocardial infarction, I: An inpatient study in Sweden. J. Psychosom. Res., 15:25 (1971).
Theorell, T., Lind, E., Fröberg, J., Karlsson, C.-G., and Levi, L.: A longitudinal study of 21 subjects with coronary heart disease – life changes, catecholamine excretion and related biochemical reactions. Psychosom. Med., (1972).
Tien, H. Y.: China's Population Struggle. Ohio State Univ. Press. Columbus (1973).
Thiessen, D. D.: Population density and behavior: A review of theoretical and physiological contributions. Texas Reports on Biology and Medicine, 22:2:266–314 (1964).
Tietze, C., Lemakau, P. and Cooper, M.: Personality disorder and spatial mobility. The Amer. Journal of Sociology, 48:29–39 (1942).
Toepfer, C. T. et al. (eds.): Environmental Psychology. MSS Information Corp., New York (1972).
Toffler, A.: Future Shock. Random House, New York (1970).
Tucker, J. and Friedman, S. T.: Population density and group size. The Amer. Journal of Sociology, 77:4:742–749 (1971).
Tumin, M. M.: Social stratification and social mobility in the development process. In Science, Technology and Development. Vol. VII: Social Problems of Development and Urbanization. United States paper prepared for the United Nations' Conference on the Application of Science and Technology for the Benefit of the Less Developed Areas, Geneva (Febr. 1963).
Tyroler, H. A. and Cassel, J.: Health consequences of culture change-II: The effect of urbanization on coronary heart mortality in rural residents. J. chron. Dis., 17:167–177 (1964).

UNICEF: Children and adolescents in slums and shanty towns in developing countries. (E/ICEF/L. 1277 and Add. 1).

United Nations: Report on international definition and measurement of standards and levels of living. A United Nations Publication, Sales No. 54.IV.5 (1954).

United Nations: Report on the World Social Situation Including Studies of Urbanization in Underdeveloped Areas. New York (1957).

United Nations: International definition and measurement of levels of living, an interim guide. A United Nations publication, Sales No. 61.IV.7 (1961).

United Nations: World population: Challenge to development. Sales No. 66.XIII.4, New York (1966).

United Nations: World Population Conference, 1965. Volumes II, III and IV. United Nations, New York (1967).

United Nations: Problems of the human environment. Report of the Secretary-General (E/4667) ECOSOC, New York (1969).

United Nations: Variables and questionnaire for comparative fertility surveys. Population Studies No. 45, Sales No.: E.69.XIII.4, New York (1970).

United Nations: Demographic Yearbook 1970. New York (1971a).

United Nations: Educational, informational, social and cultural aspects of environmental issues. Report of the Secretary-General (A/CONF. 48/9). Provisional agenda (1971b).

Untied Nations: Human Fertility and National Development. Sales No.: E.71.II.A.12, New York (1971c).

United Nations: The world population situation in 1970. Population studies No. 49, Sales No.: E.71.XIII.4, New York (1971d).

United Nations: Planning and management of human settlements for environmental quality. Report of the Secretary-General (A/CONF 48/6). Provisional agenda (1971e).

United Nations: Social indicators for housing and urban development. Report of the Ad. Hoc. group of experts (ST/ECA/173). New York (1973a).

United Nations: World housing survey. Report of the Secretary-General (E/C.6/129). Committee on Housing, Building and Planning, Geneva, Oct. 15–26 (1973b).

United Nations: Some issues relating to population distribution policies. (E/CONF 60/SYM III/21). Paper presented at ECOSOC Symposium on Population, Resources and Environment, Stockholm Sept. 25–Oct. 5, (1973c).

United Nations: Report of the Symposium on Population, Resources and Environment, Stockholm Sept. 25–Oct. 5, (1973d).

United Nations: Report of the Secretary-General on the draft world population plan of action, second draft. (E/CN. 9/292/Rev. 1) Jan. 23, (1974).

Unsigned: Hygienic aspects of urbanization. Abstracts of papers for an international conferece held in Prague, September (1971).

Unsigned: Regional Planning – A European Problem. Report of the Consultative Assembly. Council of Europe, Strasbourg (1968).

Varela, J. A.: Psychological Solutions to Social Problems. Acad. Press, Inc., New York and London (1971).

Walker Jr. B.: Health hazards associated with urbanization and over-population. Journal of the National Medical Association. 62:4:259–264 (1970).

Wall, W. D. and Williams, H. L.: Longitudinal Studies and the Social Sciences. Heynemann, London (1970).

Wallace, B.: People Their Needs, Environment, Ecology: Essays in Social Biology. Volume I. Prentice-Hall Inc., Englewood Cliffs, N. J. (1972).

Ward, B. and Dubos, R.: Only One Earth. Penguin Books Ltd, Harmondsworth, Middlesex (1972).

Warner, A. W., Morse, D. and Conney, T. E. (eds.): The Environment of Change. Colombia Univ. Press, New York and London (1969).

Weaver, G. L.-P.: Adjusting rural people to an urban environment. In Science, Technology and Development Vol. VII: Social Problems of Development and Urbanization. United States paper prepared for the United Nations Conference on the Application of Science and Technology for the Benefit of the Less Developed Areas, Geneva (Febr. 1963).

Welch, B. L.: Psychophysiological response to the mean level of environmental stimulation: A theory of environmental integration. In Symposium on Medical Aspects of Stress in the Military Climate, pp. 39–96. Walter Reed Army Institute of Research, Washington (1964).

Welch, B. L. and Welch, A. S.: Physiological Effects of Noise. Plenum Press, New York and London (1970).

Wessen, A. F.: The role of migrant studies in epidemiological research. Israel J. med. Sci., 7:12:1584–1591 (1971).

WHO: Bibliography on social and environmental influences in mental health. World Health Organization, Regional Office for Europe, Copenhagen EURO 0333 (undated).

WHO: Measurement of levels of health. Technical Report Series No. 137, Genève (1957).

WHO: Background document based on summary reports received from countries for reference and use at the technical discussions on "the challenge to public health of urbanization", prepared by Senn, Ch. L. and Ferguson, Th. (A 20/Technical discussions/1), (1967a).

WHO: Report of the technical discussions at the twentieth world health assembly on "the challenge to public health of urbanization". (A 20/Technical discussions/6). May 17, (1967b).

WHO: Urbanization as a challenge to public health. Mental health aspects, WPR/PHA/13 (1967c).

WHO: Health Hazards of the Human Environment. World Health Organization, Geneva (1972).

WHO: Environmental and health monitoring in occupational health. Technical report series, No. 535, Geneva (1973a).

WHO: Environmental deterioration and population (E/CONF. 60/SYM III/17). Paper prepared for ECOSOC Symposium on Population, Resources and Environment, Stockholm Sept. 25–Oct. 5 (1973b).

WHO: Etude collaborative Sénégal IR-0656. Santé et migration rurale – urbaine: Adaptation des migrants serer à la vie urbaine de Dkar. (SHS/73.1) Geneva (1973c).

WHO: Suggested outline for use by countries in discussing "the role of health services in preserving or restoring the full effectiveness of the human environment in the promotion of health" (OMH/73.2) (1973d).

WHO: Health aspects of population trends and prospects. Working paper No. 8 for the World Population Conference, 1974 (FH/73. 1 Rev. 1) Draft (1973e).

WHO: Background document based on replies received form countries for reference and use at the technical discussions on "the role of the health services in preserving or restoring the full effectiveness of the human environment in the promotion of health" (A 27/Technical discussions/1), (1974a).

WHO: The role of the health services in preserving or restoring the full effectiveness of human environment in the promotion of health. Report of the technical discussion at the twenty-seventh world health assembly (A27/Technical discussion/6), (1974b).

Wilner, D. M., Walkley, A. P. and Tayback, M.: How does the quality of housing affect health and family adjustment? Amer. J. publ. Health, 46:736–744 (1956).

Winsborough, H. H.: The social consequences of high population density. Law and Contemporary Problems, 30:120–126 (1965).

Wohlwill, J. F.: The physical environment: A problem for a psychology of stimulation Journal of Social Issues, 22:4:29–37 (1966).

Wolf, S.: Medical problems of modern society, urbanization and stress. Unpublished manuscript. (Undated).

Wolf, S.: Psychosocial forces in myocardial infarction and sudden death. In *Levi, L. (ed.):* Society, Stress and Disease: The Psychosocial Environment and Psychosomatic Diseases, pp. 324–330. Oxford Univ. Press, London, New York, Toronto (1971).

Wolf, S. and Goodell, H. (eds.): Harold G. Wolff's Stress and Disease, 2nd Edition. Charles C. Thomas Publisher, Springfield, I11. (1968).

Wolfe, S. W.: Avoid sickness – How life change affects your health. Family Circle, 5:30:166–170 (1972).

Wolff, K. (ed.): Social and Cultural Factors in Mental Health and Mental Illness. Charles C. Thomas Publisher, Springfield, I11. (1971).

Wolpert, J.: Migration as an adjustment to environmental stress. Journal of Social Issues, 22:4:92–102 (1966).

World Bank: Urbanization. Sector working paper (1972).

World Bank: Trends in developing countries. Washington (1973a).

World Bank: World bank atlas. Washington (1973b).

Wynne-Edwards, V. C.: Animal Dispersion in Relation to Social Behavior. Oliver and Boyd, London (1962).

Yancey, W. L.: Architecture, interaction, and social control. The case of a large-scale public housing project. Environment and Behavior, 3:3–21 (1971).

Youmans, E. G.: Family disengagement among older urban and rural women. Journal of Gerontology, 22:209–211 (1967).

Zimbardo, P. G.: The human choice: individuation, reason, and order versus deindividuation, impulse and chaos. In *Arnold, W. J. (ed.):*

Nebraska Symposium on Motivation, pp. 237—307. Nebr. (1969).
Zwingman, CH. and Pfister-Ammende, M. (eds.): Uprooting and after. . .
Springer-Verlag, New York (1973).

Ødegaard, Ø.: Emigration and insanity. Acta Psychiat. et Neur., Suppl. 4
(1932).
Ödmann, E. and Dahlberg, G.-B.: Urbanization in Sweden. Means and
Methods for the Planning. Allmänna förlaget, Uddevalla (1970).
Örtendahl, C.: Olikstora orter och kommunal service — En granskning av
väljarnas attityder i två intervjuundersökningar. In SOU:1974:2 Ortsbundna Levnadsvillkor. Allmänna förlaget, Stockholm (1974).

10 Glossary of technical terms

Adrenal cortex (adj. *adrenocortical*) — the thick parenchymatous layer enclosing the medulla of the adrenal gland; secretes cortisol and other corticosteroids.

Adrenal glands — two small ductless glands, one located above each kidney and consisting of cortex and medulla.

Adrenal medulla (adj. *medullary*) — the highly vascular mass of chromaffin tissue forming the center of an adrenal gland; secretes adrenaline and noradrenaline.

Adrenaline (= epinephrine) — one of the "stress hormones" produced by the adrenal medulla.

Catecholamines — a compound of catechol and amine, e.g. adrenaline and noradrenaline.

Cholesterol — the principal animal sterol, found in small amounts in many tissues, occurring notably in bile, gallstones, the brain, blood cells, plasma, egg yolk.

Coronary — encircling, as either of two arteries that supply blood directly to the heart tissues. Loosely, of or pertaining to the heart.

Corticosteroids — hormones from the adrenal cortex; glucocorticosteroids acting on the metabolism of carbohydrates and mineralcorticosteroids influencing the retention and excretion of salt and water.

Cybernetics — the theoretical study of control process in biological and other systems, especially the mathematical analysis of the flow of information in such systems.

Cyclic psychoses — affective disorders characterized by periodic mood variations between the poles of cheerfulness and sadness.

Ecology — the scientific study of the interrelations of living organisms and the non-living elements of their environment.

Ecosystem — the fundamental unit in ecology, comprising the living organisms and the non-living elements interacting in a certain defined area.

Endocrine glands (= ductless glands) — glands not having excretory ducts; they secrete their substances, hormones, directly into the blood stream.

Epidemiology — the scientific study of factors that influence the frequency and distribution of diseases in groups of people.

Ethology — the scientific study of animal behaviour.

Etiology — the science dealing with the causation of disease.

Gastrointestinal — pertaining to stomach and intestine.

Hyperventilation — abnormally fast or deep respiration in which excessive quantities of air are taken in, causing buzzing in the ears, tingling of extremities, and sometimes fainting.

Hypochondriasis — persistent neurotic conviction that one is or is likely to become ill.

Hypophysis (adj. *hypophyseal*) — the pituitary gland, an important endocrine gland connected to the base of the brain by a stalk. Its secretions control the other endocrine glands.

Hypothalamus — lowest part of the middle brain, contains the centres of the two parts of the autonomic nervous system: the sympathetic and parasympathetic, respectively.

Natality — the same as birth rate.

Neurosis (adj. *neurotic*) — a collective name for less incapacitating nervous diseases: (a) psychoneuroses with primarily mental symptoms, and (b) organ neuroses with primarily physical symptoms.

Noradrenaline (= norepinephrine) — one of the hormones of the adrenal medulla and the sympathetic nervous system.

Palpitation — rapid beating of the heart.

Pathogen (adj. *pathogenic)* — any disease producing agent.

Peptic ulcer — one on the mucous membrane of stomach or duodenum (the beginning portion of the small intestine).

Peristalsis — a wavelike progression of alternate contraction and relaxation of the muscle fibers of tubular organs, by which contents are propelled along e.g. the alimentary tract.

Phylogeny (adj. *phylogenic)* — the complete developmental history of a race or groups of organisms.

Physiology — the science of the normal functions of the bodily organs.

Psychiatry — the branch of medicine that deals with diseases of the mind.

Psychomotor — pertaining to motor effects of cerebral or psychic activity.

Psychosis — a major emotional disorder with derangement of the personality and loss of contact with reality, often with delusions, hallucinations or illusions.

Psychosomatic — from *psyche,* mind and *soma,* body: the theory and methods of medicine based upon the mind-body relationship, in various diseases.

Puerperium — the state of a woman while bearing a child or immediately thereafter.

Rheumatoid arthritis — a chronic disease marked by stiffness and inflammation of the joints, weakness, loss of mobility, and deformity.

Soma — body, bodily processes.

Sympathotonia — a condition in which the sympathetic nervous system closely integrated with its partner, the parasympathetic, with which it controls, among other things, the functioning of our internal organs.

Sympathotonia — a condition in which the sympathetic nervous system dominates the general functioning of the body organs.

Tachycardia — excessively rapid heart-beat.

Teratogen — an agent or influence that causes physical defects in the developing fetus.

Thyroxine — a hormone of the thyroid gland.

Vasomotor — having an effect on the caliber of blood vessels.

Vasovagal syncope — a faint due to temporary cerebral anemia.

Vegetative — concerned with growth and nutrition; functioning involuntarily and unconsciously.

Index

Parker, 68, 81
Paticipation, 92
Pathogen, 132
Pathology, 86
Peptic ulcer, 72, 132
Perception of reality, 13
Peristalsis, 132
Perrins, 81
Persecution, 36
Personal,
  conflict, 36
  factors, 15
  habits, revision of, 22
  safety, 62, 64
Personality disorders, 74
Peru, 57
Pfister-Ammende, 35
Philippines, 57, 58
Phylogenetic, 15, 21, 132
Phylogeny, 132
Physical,
  activity, 21, 77
  limitations, 27
  planning, 93
  setting, 11
  stimuli, 16–18, 38
  structure, 97
Physiology, 132
Planet eating, 101, 104, 106
P.O.W. captivity, 36
Political,
  process, 62
  resources, 61
Pollutants, 64
Polluted air, 78
Pollution, 27, 43, 44, 78, 96, 103–105
Population, 16, 17
  density, 19, 30, 65, 66, 75, 78, 80,
  81, 86, 92, 102, 104
  density and change, 18, 22, 23, 38,
  87, 97
  density and change, in urban and rural
  settings, 24
  density, changes in, 31
  density, high, 29
  density, levels and changes in, 12, 100,
  density, levels of, 29
  density, rapid increase in, 86
  density, rise in, 27
  explosion, 24, 51, 101, 106
  growth, 25, 29, 44, 48, 49, 53, 54, 56,
  100–104
  structures, 44
  structures and processes, 16, 17, 24
  variables, 97, 99
Portugal, 58

Poverty, 42, 53, 58, 100–102, 105, 106
Power, 92
Precursors, 97, 104
  of disease, 15, 17, 18, 20, 21, 23
Pregnancy, 22, 87
Prematurity, 87
Preventive action, 97
Privacy, 98
  lack of, 83
  preclusion of, 82
Production, 54
Professionals, 36
Prosecution, 68
Prospective intervention community
  studies, 99
Protein, 27
  supply, 58
Psychiatric,
  disorders, 74
  hospitals, 78
Psychiatry, 132
Psychobiological,
  program, 15–17, 20
  programming, 38, 49
Psychological stimulation, 79
Psychomotor, 132
  activities, 21
Psychoneurotic, 20
Psychosis, 74, 132
Psychosocial, 74, 104
  environment, 46
  environmental medicine, 13
  factors, 11, 85, 91, 94, 95
  limitations, 27
  setting, 11
  stimuli, 15–19, 21, 22, 38
  stressors, 15, 22
Psychosomatic, 132
  and social pathology, 86
  disorders, 59, 97, 103
Public service, 67, 93
Puerperium, 87, 132

Quality of life, 11–13, 16–19, 36, 40,
  43, 44, 46, 47, 51, 53–55, 59, 61,
  64, 65, 67, 69, 78, 82, 86, 89–92,
  94, 96, 97, 99, 100, 102–106
Querido, 29, 85

Radford, 92
Rahe, 22
Rank order, 82
Rape, 75
Ratner, 77
Recreation, 48, 61
Recreational opportunities, 103